# OVERCOMING

# BLOCKS

# TO HEALING

*Foundational Truths for the Ministry of Healing*

**Bill Banks**

*Overcoming Blocks to Healing* by Bill Banks
ISBN # 0-89228-136-7

Editor: Stephen P. Banks


Copyright ©, 2002
**Impact Christian Books, Inc**.
332 Leffingwell Ave.,
Kirkwood, MO 63122
314-822-3309

Cover Design: *Ideations*


All Scripture references are taken from
*The Authorized King James Version.*

**Printed in the United States of America**

## DEDICATION

To all true seekers of Truth.

Especially **to those** who have been attempting to stand in faith, believing for a miracle of healing. The truths in this book relate to receiving from God in other areas, but the primary focus of this writing is *healing*.

And with gratitude **to the Holy Spirit** who is the revealer of these, as of all Godly truths.

\* \* \*

## Titles by the Same Author

*Alive Again!*   5.95

*Ministering to Abortion's Aftermath*   5.95

*Power for Deliverance: Songs of Deliverance*   5.95

*Deliverance from Fat*   5.95

*Deliverance from Childlessness*   5.95

*Deliverance For Children & Teens*   6.95

*Breaking Unhealthy Soul-Ties*   7.95

*Shame-Free*   7.95

*The Little Skunk*  (Sue Banks)   10.99

*Everything Is Possible With God*   9.95
(The Martin Hlastan Story)

*How to Tap into the Wisdom of God*   10.95

*The Heavens Declare...*   8.95

*Three Kinds of Faith of Faith for Healing*   4.95

*Overcoming Blocks to Healing*   9.99

# TABLE OF CONTENTS

*A Fellow Traveler*                                          7
*Foreword*                                                   9
*Author's Introduction*                                     11

Chapter 1
God's Will Regarding Healing.................................1

Chapter 2
God's Will Was Expressed in the Atonement ..........17

Chapter Three
Satan's Will Regarding Healing ...........................31

Chapter 4
The Role of Man in Healing.........................49

Chapter 5
"Could it Be God's Will for Me to Die?".................65

Chapter 6
"Could *They* Be Right?"...................................83

Chapter 7
"What about Paul's Thorn in the Flesh?".................99

Chapter 8
"And What about Job?"...................................121

Chapter 9
"Do I Have Enough Faith?".....................129

Chapter 10
"How Desperate Are You?"......................149

Chapter 11
"What About Doctors and Medicine?"....................153

Chapter 12
"Is It Time For My Healing?"............................163

Chapter 13
"Is Bad Theology Killing You?"........................175

Chapter 14
"Could I Have a Pride Block?"...........................199

Chapter 15
Blatant Sin Blocks Healing ...................................... 207

Chapter 16
Unexpected Blocks ..............................................219

Chapter 17
Conclusion: "Is There Always a Block?"...............225


*Appendix A - Have You Received The Baptism With the Holy Spirit?*.................................................................. 233
*Appendix B - Specific Superatural Healings in Scripture*......235

# A Fellow Traveler

*Many years ago, I heard the following story. Perhaps it affected me so much because I was the son of an immigrant, or perhaps it was because of the beautiful truth, which my Heavenly Father placed within it.*

In the old country, there lived a man who wanted to emigrate to America, the land of promise. He worked very hard and saved every penny he could from his meager income, until finally late in life, he had accumulated enough to pay for his passage. He quit his job and went to the steamship office, and there he proudly laid his money on the counter and purchased passage on a passenger steamship. After paying for his fare, there was just barely enough left to buy a tin of crackers and a large piece of cheese, so that he would have something to eat during the crossing, which would take about a week.

Each day when the other passengers filed into one of the large dining rooms on the ship for their meals, he would take his cheese and crackers and eat alone on the deck. Finally on the last day of the journey, as an expectant crowd began gathering on deck and just before they came in sight of the Statue of Liberty, a woman approached the man and addressed him.

"Excuse me, sir, I do not wish to pry, but I must ask you a question."

"Certainly, madame, what is it that you wish to know?" He replied politely.

"I have noticed that each day, while everyone else goes to the dining room, you sit alone on the deck eating your cheese and crackers. Why is that?"

Embarrassed, the old man explained his story of scrimping and saving for twenty years until he had managed to accumulate the fare for his trip to the land of promise, and that he had no money left for food, except the paltry sum he had spent for his crackers and cheese.

Shocked, the woman exclaimed, "You mean no one told you that all your meals were included in the price of your ticket?"

* * *

How many Christians are there, today, on their journey to the Promised Land, who are living only on cheese and crackers, because they too are unaware that Jesus has already provided a feast for them – everything His children could ever need was included in the price of their "salvation-ticket"?

This man was prevented from enjoying life to the fullest, because he had *a block*: he was unaware of all that was available to him.

> *But seek ye first the kingdom of God, and his righteousness; and **all these things** shall be added unto you.*　　　　　　　　　　　　Mat. 6:33

# Foreword

I highly recommend that you <u>read</u> this book carefully, <u>reflect</u> on the insights presented, and <u>use</u> what you learn about God's healing power in your personal ministry.

It has been my delight to know the author, Bill Banks and his wife Sue, for over 35 years. I vividly recall visiting his bedside during the fall of 1970 as his cancer-filled body was wasting away. When Jesus healed Bill completely from terminal cancer, many of us were thrilled and amazed. His healing built up my own faith and directly inspired me to pursue and subsequently receive the baptism of the Holy Spirit, which supercharged my Christian faith. Bill's life also changed dramatically as a result of his healing. He left a successful profession in the insurance industry and moved into a full time Christian ministry involving teaching, writing, publishing, conducting seminars, leading weekly Bible studies, and praying for people's needs in a prayer room adjoining his office.

Over the years, Bill has been a consistent pursuer of practical applications for God's Word and has learned much about healing from personal experience and from praying for others. As a result, thousands of people have received a gift of healing from Jesus over the three decades of Bill's ministry. In this book, he writes with clarity and wit telling dramatic, true-life stories of healings and then providing Scriptural text relevant to each situation. Bill's insights will challenge and quicken your faith.

Having always kept up our friendship and living only a few miles away from each other ever since his healing in 1970, I can confirm Bill's continuing dedication to our Lord Jesus Christ, and I am personally acquainted with some of the people in the healing stories he describes. I have heard him teach with powerful results, I have read many of his books, and I have been to his prayer room. You should also know that Bill's commitment to Christ extends well beyond writing and speaking. Despite never having a formal fund raising program, his ministry helps support annual inner-city food projects, a church and an orphanage in Haiti, missionaries in Russia and Eastern Europe, plus extensive Christian literature distributions to prisoners and cancer patients.

You will find this book is a treasure that clarifies: 1) God's will regarding healing, 2) Jesus' complete work on the cross, 3) Satan's strategies for interfering with God's will, and 4) what you can do to counter Satan's interference and begin to live in health.


> Charles F. Fay, President
> Clayton Missouri Chapter
> Full Gospel Business Men's Fellowship, Int'l.

# Author's Introduction

In this book I will share with you the major questions and blocks that confronted me, before I was healed of a terminal illness, and the answers which I discovered to those questions. Fortunately I did find them, and was led subsequently into a ministry of healing, which has lasted over thirty years. I also offer herein comments and insights on the other questions, or blocks, that I have encountered in those who have come to see me over the yeaers seeking prayer for healing.

Although we are technically talking about blocks to healing, many of these blocks are equally valid in other areas of our warfare with Satan. Therefore, many of the truths dealt with will transcend the issue of healing.

Far too many of us have allowed our theology to be either shaped, or influenced, by experiences – our own and those of others. For example, insurance companies have defined certain tragedies as "acts of God": a tornado, a flood, a hurricane may destroy property and kill many people. Insurance companies may deny coverage, labeling these occurrences as "acts of God." Regrettably, modern man has bought into this lie, and it comes from the Devil; these are not acts of God! They may not be insurable incidents, but they are definitely not acts of God: God does not kill innocent people. He does not even take any pleasure in the death of the wicked as He informs us in Ezekiel.

*For I have no pleasure in the death of him that dieth, saith the Lord GOD: wherefore turn yourselves, and live ye.*                                    Ezek. 18:32

A few months ago while I was teaching on blocks to healing at a men's retreat, a young man asked a very good question: "Is there always a block when someone isn't healed?"

I answered honestly, "I cannot say that there *always is*. However, I always suspect that there is a block, even if I may not have the discernment to see it, nor the answer for it. I operate on the premise that there has not been a power failure in heaven."

God is still the healer, regardless of my specific experiences, and His promises are still completely true, even if I am not experiencing all that he has promised. If I am not, the question is simply "Why not?" That is what we hope to uncover in the following pages.

Almost daily since I was healed of termnal cancer, I have had the opportunity and privilege of ministering to sick and needy Christians. Many of them have been Christians, who as the result of a dire need, often cancer, suddenly have become aware of the deficiency of their understanding about healing, a subject to which approximately *a third* of the Gospels is devoted.

Recently while ministering to a young man seeking healing for his wife who had inoperable, terminal cancer, he asked me to help him answer questions which he had in his own mind, as well as the various objections raised to healing by his minister, and well meaning evangelical friends.

It suddenly struck me that we have been blessed with those answers and have been teaching them for more than thirty years. Furthermore, we have seen them bring life to the hearers. Yet, most of the Christian world is still at the starting point as far as the issue of healing goes. The ministerial leadership in many churches and a good number of well meaning sincere Christians are still asking the basic, fundamental, "kindergarten" questions, because no one has satisfactorily answered those questions for them. Many, who have been in ministry as long as we have, are still asking the same "beginning questions" that I was asking over thirty years ago, when I was trying to discover God's will for healing! I do recognize that there are many faithful and devoted servants of God, who may not believe fully in healing, because of their tradition, training and even experience. However, I believe that, if they will carefully consider the points made in this book with hearts open before God, He will broaden their horizons and reveal His truth to them.

Unfortunately, many good men have been stunted by their denomination's position on healing and have allowed the 'blinders' of "tradition" to prevent them from seeing God's truth. "By your traditions ye have made my words of none effect!" (Mk. 7:13)

Many others have innocently assumed that since the questions that they posed were not answered to their satisfaction, there simply were no answers, and so they have locked themselves into positions, which they now hold, or rather which *hold them* like a steel trap. It's been said some men have minds like steel traps: "Closed and rusty!"

I don't wish to sound unkind, but the Scripture also admonishes those who should have studied and learned, but have been lax.

*For when for the time ye ought to be teachers, ye have need that one teach you again which be the first principles of the oracles of God; and are become such as have need of milk, and not of strong meat.*

Heb. 5:12

This situation is much like that which prevailed in my Sunday School class, when I was a child, and a new substitute teacher showed up. Recognizing that the best defense was a good offense, someone would immediately ask the new teacher, something like this, "What about the *good* heathen, who haven't heard about Jesus?"

The teachers, invariably caught off guard, spluttered about, trying to come up with an answer, or often just took off on a tangent, ignoring the question. Regrettably, our questions were not motivated by true compassion for the poor heathen, but rather, intended as a diversion to avoid exposing our own ignorance, should the teacher begin asking *us* questions. Many of the students unfortunately assumed that there really weren't any good answers, or that the church didn't have them, and settled into playing this particular "religious game." Perhaps we were also too lazy to research the subject for ourselves; in any event, the results were the same.

I desire to share with you, truths and answers that I feel the Lord has revealed through years of serious consideration of these issues. These answers may not be complete, nor satisfy every facet of one's curiosity – but I feel for the serious seeker of truth, they will either provide the answers that you desire, or else a sound foundation for the complete answers, which the Holy Spirit may grant, or "quicken," to you.

I will be satisfied and feel that my task has been accomplished in obedience, if you find healing, find answers to some of your questions, find new understanding, and even find that your faith has been stimulated and challenged. May you be caused to seek Him, who has all Truth, and Who desires to reveal Himself to you in all His fullness.

**Bill Banks**

# Chapter 1

# What Is God's Will Regarding Healing?

### "Everything That Happens Is According to His Will, Isn't It?"

Everyone who seeks God during a time of illness faces the question of God's will. I was one of those strategically blocked by the familiar concept of *"Thy will be done."* If I was sick, then it must be by His design, His will. I did not know at that time that His will is for *all* to be healed.

Initially, I wasn't able to pray through what I described as 'the steel shield' over my mind caused by the thought behind the phrase, "Thy will be done." Many quote this in regard to healing, and in a specific manner: "Thy will be done. On earth as it is in heaven." As such they have made the mistake of putting a period where a comma belongs: "Thy will be done, on earth *as it is in heaven.*" And in heaven there is no pain, no suffering, no cancer, no tumors, no diabetes, no death! God's will is manifested in heaven, perfectly. This implies that it is God's will for all forms of sickness to be absent from His creation on earth, *as it is in heaven.* This is truly a marvelous revelation.

The Lord used two particular Scriptures to help me conquer this objection, and I will discuss these in detail (as explained in Luke 5:12-13 in this Chapter, and later in Luke 13:11-16 in Chapter 3.)

I had mistakenly assumed that if God wanted to heal me, He would. However, if all mankind were to follow the same logic, no one would accept Jesus, no one would take

1

the steps which David referred to in Psalms, "to call on the name of the Lord." Instead, they would assume that God would automatically save them, *if He wanted to do so*. On both issues He has made Himself abundantly clear: *we* have a part to play.

First, in salvation, we are to confess and to believe,

> *That if **thou shalt confess** with thy mouth the Lord Jesus, and **shalt believe** in thine heart that God hath raised him from the dead, thou shalt be saved.*
>
> Rom. 10:9

And second, in healing, we are to ask for faith-filled prayer from other believers. Thus even in healing, man has a role.

> *Is any sick among you? **let him call** for the elders of the church; and let them pray over him, anointing him with oil in the name of the Lord:*     James 5:14

It is crucial for us to know and understand God's will for us, for our physical as well as our spiritual lives. Perhaps the most common block for people is the foundational question...

### "Is It God's Will to Heal?"

This we can resolve up front. Yes, it is His will to heal. Not because I say so, but because *God* has said so: He first identified Himself as our Healer, in Exodus 15, when He established a covenant of healing. The Scriptures which follow clearly establish His will on the subject..

> ... ***I am the LORD that healeth thee***.     Exo. 15:26

2

*And ye shall serve the LORD your God, and he shall bless thy bread, and thy water; and **I will take sickness away** from the midst of thee.* Exo. 23:25

Probably the next most significant question is:
## "Does God Want To Heal Everyone?"

*Bless the LORD, O my soul, and forget not all his benefits: Who forgiveth all thine iniquities; who **healeth all thy diseases**;* Psa. 103:2-3

God not only healed all, but in addition, *promised* that we will be restored in order to serve Him energetically.

*...thy youth is renewed like the eagle's.* Psa. 103:5b

*Because he hath set his love upon me, therefore will I deliver him: I will set him on high, because he hath known my name. He shall call upon me, and I will answer him: I will be with him in trouble; I will deliver him, and honour him. With **long life** will I satisfy him, and show him my salvation.* Psa. 91:14-16

In the 91st Psalm, we see the Christian pictured as victorious, no longer under Satan's dominion but rather on the offensive against Satan's activity. The words of this Psalm are paralled in Luke 10:19

*Thou shalt tread upon the lion and adder: the young lion and the dragon shalt thou trample under feet.*
Psa. 91:13

*Behold, I give unto you power to tread on serpents and scorpions, and over all the power of the enemy: and nothing shall by any means hurt you.* Luke 10:19

3

Clearly, it is His will to heal others, and to be victorious over all that comes against His people.

In a similar sense there is a parallel between our lives and the Old Covenant sacrifices of the nation of Israel. The sacrifices offered to God by the priesthood were to be without blemish. The Lord in fact, chastised the Israelites for bringing sick and wounded animals as sacrifices in His temple (Mal. 1:8).

If God in the Old Testament required that the lambs to be sacrificed in His temple had to be *without spot or blemish*, how much more is Jesus, *the Good Shepherd*, concerned about the sheep of *His own flock*. Paul seems to imply these thoughts when he writes: *I pray God your whole spirit and soul and body be preserved **blameless**...*(I Thes. 5:23a) and...*that ye present your bodies a living **sacrifice**, **holy**, **acceptable** unto God...* (Rom. 12:1). Our lives are to be the *spiritual sacrifices* without blemish, which replace the *physical sacrifices* of old.

However, on a more personal basis, and more to the point:

## "Is It God's Will To Heal *Me?*"

Jesus answered that question for you, and for me, when He answered it for a leper, as recorded in the fifth chapter of Luke, and in Matthew 8:3. This leper was also clearly in doubt as to Jesus' will to heal him, and asked almost the same question, when he stated, "Lord, *if thou wilt* [if it is your will, desire, intent to do so] thou canst make me clean." In other words, "If you *want* to do so," "if you *will* to do it," "if it's your will to heal me, you can make me whole; you can make me clean of my leprosy."

> *And Jesus put forth his hand, and touched him, saying, **I will**; be thou clean. And immediately his leprosy was cleansed.*　　　　　　　Mat. 8:3

4

Jesus not only states it to be His will to heal, but also supernaturally confirmed His words with dramatic proof: the *leper was healed!* However, the man wasn't healed until he asked: *asking* was a part of the healing process. We'll learn more about this later.

### "Did Jesus Heal Everyone?"

What is Jesus' will, or intent, regarding healing for everyone? Just as salvation is for whosoever will receive the Savior, so healing is available for *all*, who would receive the Healer. Healing is for *any* and for *every* individual, and for *any* and *every manner* of sickness disease or affliction.

The entire earthly ministry of Jesus bears adequate testimony to His will to heal all who needed and desired healing.

> *And Jesus went about all Galilee, teaching in their synagogues, and preaching the gospel of the kingdom, and **healing all manner of sickness** and **all manner of disease** among the people. And his fame went throughout all Syria: and they brought unto him **all sick people** that were taken with divers diseases and torments, and those which were possessed with devils, and those which were lunatic, and those that had the palsy; and **he healed them**.* Mat. 4:23-24

> *But when Jesus knew it, he withdrew himself from thence: and great multitudes followed him, and **he healed them all**;* Mat. 12:15

For some reason, many have difficulty picturing the God of the Old Testament as the loving Heavenly Father whom Jesus described. Theremore, we want to clearly establish that there is perfect hamony within the Godhead.

5

## "Is it the Will of the Father to Heal?"

Jesus was the perfect manifestation of the Father's will. He said of Himself,

*Lo, I come to **do thy will**, O God.*     Heb. 10:9a

*Jesus saith unto them, My meat is **to do the will of him that sent me**, and to finish his work.*
                                                    John 4:34

Jesus and the Father were in perfect agreement concerning their will for mankind and this means a shared desire for the well being and healing of their created beings. If Jesus healed, then it was the Father's will for Him to do so.  Their wills were one:

*Even so it is not the **will of your Father** which is in heaven, that one of these little ones should perish.*
                                                    Mat. 18:14

*But Jesus answered them, My Father worketh hitherto, and I work.   Then answered Jesus and said unto them, Verily, verily, I say unto you, The Son can do nothing of himself, but what he seeth the Father do: for what things soever he doeth, these also **doeth the Son likewise**.*                    John 5:17-19

Sicknesses, including fever, crippling disease, legions of demons and even death, could not remain in the presence of Jesus.

From Calvary's cross Jesus gave His own commentary and summary of His life and work:

*...It is finished...*                              John 19:30

6

What was it that was finished? The work that the Father had sent Him to perform.

*Jesus saith unto them, My meat is to do the will of him that sent me, and **to finish his work**.*
John 4:34

### "Is Healing the Will of the Holy Spirit?"

The Godhead is in perfect unity on the issue of healing, Father, Son and Holy Spirit. Each Member works in agreement with the others to bring wholeness to the people of God.

*And it came to pass on a certain day, as he was teaching, that there were Pharisees and doctors of the law sitting by, which were come out of every town of Galilee, and Judaea, and Jerusalem: and **the power** [Grk. dunamis, dynamite power promised to believers; a representation of the Holy Spirit] **of the Lord** was present to heal them.*
Luke 5:17

*But if the Spirit of him that raised up Jesus from the dead dwell in you, he that raised up Christ from the dead shall also **quicken your mortal bodies by his Spirit** that dwelleth in you.*
Rom. 8:11

*Through mighty signs and wonders, by **the power** of **the Spirit of God**...*
Rom. 15:19a

Not only is the Godhead in complete agreement on the issue of healing, but so also are God's agents. We see this in the numerous men of God, who wrote the core texts of the Bible.

## Witnesses Who Confirmed Healing to Be within God's Will:

The **Apostle John**, conditioned health upon the prospering of one's soul.

> *Beloved, I wish* [or, lit. "I pray"] *above all things that thou mayest prosper and **be in health**, even as thy soul prospereth.*                              3 John 1:2

The **Prophet Isaiah** relates health to a God-pleasing fast.

> *Is not this the fast that I have chosen?...Then shall thy light break forth as the morning, and **thine health shall spring forth speedily:** and thy righteousness shall go before thee; the glory of the LORD shall be thy rereward.*                              Isa. 58:6-8

The **Apostle James**, exorted prayer for the sick.

> *Confess your faults one to another, and pray one for another, that ye may **be healed**. The effectual fervent prayer of a righteous man availeth much.*
>                              James 5:16

The **Apostle Peter,** references Isaiah.

> *Who his own self bare our sins in his own body on the tree, that we, being dead to sins, should live unto righteousness: by whose stripes ye were **healed**.*
>                              1 Pet. 2:24

## "But Everybody Knows God Doesn't Heal Everyone."
"Whom specifically has God refused to heal?" I often

ask. Many ministers have confronted me with this objection. My old 'flesh-man' loves to ask them, "How many people, whom you have anointed with oil and prayed for publicly for healing, has God refused to heal?" They usually mumble and splutter, "Why we have *never* anointed anyone with oil in *our* church." Then, how dare they accuse God of not honoring His word, when they haven't even given Him the opportunity to do so?

I quote the entitre passage from James mentioned earlier, because it is so important and foundational. It gives the only Scriptural instructions for a sick Christian. I was told by a theologian that when he asked his professor in Seminary how they handled James 5 and the anointing with oil, the reply was, "We skip over it."

> *Is any sick among you? let him call for the elders of the church; and let them pray over him, anointing him with oil in the name of the Lord: And the prayer of faith shall save the sick, and the Lord shall raise him up; and if he have committed sins, they shall be forgiven him. Confess your faults one to another, and pray one for another, that ye may **be healed**. The effectual fervent prayer of a righteous man availeth much.* James 5:14-16

Consider also all the instances recorded just by Matthew, where Jesus healed not only individuals, but also multitudes of people (Mat. 4:23; 9:35; 12:15; 14:36; 19:2; 21:14) and all the occasions when they brought **all their sick** to Jesus to be healed (Mat. 4:24; 8:16; 9:2,32; 12:22; 14:35; 17:16) and He **healed them all!**

**All these Scriptural precedents leave no room for any type of sickness or disease allowed by God, or intended by Him for man to bear!**

9

## "I Don't Want to Pray Against God's Will"

It's really rather farfetched and presumptuous to assume that we are capable of causing God to do something that is not His will. God never has done, and never will do, anything contrary to his will.

When we pray for healing, we are praying for *the fulfillment of the will* of God expressed in His multifold promises for healing, as recorded in His written Word.

## "My Minister Says to Pray, 'Heal Me, *If* It Be Thy Will.'"

It is perfectly acceptable to pray for a revelation or expression of God's will in areas not spoken of in His word, but in those areas where He has already stated His will, it is insulting to do so. It is like saying, *"If* you really want me to stay saved, then give me a sign." He has already given you the life of His Son, and sixty-six books expressing His will on that subject.

Using "if" is a cop-out, and a loop-hole, indicating a lack of faith, and it has been used by powerless and faith-weak ministers and people as a means of covering themselves in the event a healing doesn't occur.

## "But Is It Still God's *Ongoing* Will To Heal Everyone, Today?"

For the answer to this question we look to the charge given to the disciples of Jesus, and to their actions following His ascension into heaven, recorded in the Book of Acts. From the passages below, it was clearly Jesus' will for His followers to continue all aspects of His ministry.

> *And when he had called unto him his twelve disciples, he gave them power against unclean spirits, to cast them out, and to heal **all** manner of sickness and **all** manner of disease.*                    Mat. 10:1

10

*Then he called his twelve disciples together, and gave them power and authority over **all** devils, and to cure diseases. And he sent them to preach the kingdom of God, and to heal the sick.*       Luke 9:2

**All these Scriptural precedents leave no room for doubt regarding the Lord's *ongoing will* toward healing!**

### Witnesses Who Allege That it Is Still God's Will to Heal Today .

It is still His ongoing will to heal as attested by the following people who healed in His name:

Jesus commissioned not only **the Disciples** and **the Twelve Apostles** but also **the Seventy-two** in Luke 10. They were told to "Heal the sick." In essence, **all His followers** were told to continue Jesus' ministry of healing:

*And these signs shall follow **them that believe**... In my name...they shall lay hands on **the sick**, and they **shall recover**.*       Mark 16:17-18

After Jesus was received up into Heaven, **His followers** continued His ministry.

*...As my Father hath sent me, even so send I you.*       John 20:21b

*And they went forth, and preached every where, the Lord working with them, and confirming the word **with signs following**. Amen.*       Mark 16:20

**Peter and John** did not have any doubt that it was still Jesus' will to heal when they met the lame man at the gate called Beautiful (Acts 3:2ff). They healed him. Nor did any

11

of the other apostles have such doubts because:

> *.... by the hands of **the apostles** were many signs and wonders wrought among the people...  There came also a multitude out of the cities round about unto Jerusalem, bringing sick folks, and them which were vexed with unclean spirits: and they **were healed every one**.*
>
> Acts 5:12a, 16

Still later, **Philip** the evangelist apparently had no doubt concerning God's will regarding healing, when he went down to Samaria:

> *And the people with one accord gave heed unto those things which Philip spake, hearing and seeing the miracles which he did. For unclean spirits, crying with loud voice, came out of many that were possessed with them: and many taken with palsies, and that were lame, **were healed**. And there was great joy in that city.*
>
> Acts 8:6-8

More than twenty-five years after Jesus's ascension, healing continued to be the will of God for His people.  The **Holy Spirit** provided, among the gifts of the Spirit enumerated in First Corinthians chapter 12, one which specifically included the gifts (plural) of healing..

> *...to another the **gifts of healing** by the same Spirit;*
>
> 1 Cor. 12:9b

Also the mere shadow of **Peter** was sufficient to bring healing to those in need.

> *Insomuch that they brought forth the sick into the streets, and laid them on beds and couches, that at*

*the least the shadow of Peter passing by might over-*
*shadow some of them. There came also a multitude*
*out of the cities round about unto Jerusalem, bring-*
*ing sick folks, and them which were vexed with un-*
*clean spirits: and they were healed every one.*

Acts 5:16

And still later **Paul** was even more uniquely used.

*And God wrought special miracles by the hands of*
*Paul: So that from his body were brought unto the*
*sick handkerchiefs or aprons, and the diseases de-*
*parted from them, and the evil spirits went out of them.*

Acts 19:11-12

In approximately 90 A.D. and roughly sixty years after the crucifixion of Jesus, **James** recorded the Scriptural prescription for a sick Christian. He also indicates in James 5:14, the passage previously considered, that sickness should not normally be the case He asked *is* there "any (one) sick among you?"

However, perhaps you are wondering, "Sure God may heal many people, but some don't get healed," and...

### "I May Be One Whom God Won't Heal."

The underlying theory in the above statement is that God is using the sickness to "teach" the ill person something, or that the person is simply not sufficiently deserving for this precious gift. The most theologically twisted argument is that God is using this sickness for His "glory." The answer again is found in Scripture.

Remember that on numerous occasions, crowds came to Jesus bringing all the sick folk from throughout the countryside. The glaring fallacy in the above arguments is that had there been a category of *ineligible candidates for heal-*

*ing*, such as those to whom God was teaching something, or for whom He had a higher purpose in their affliction, surely someone would have made a mistake and brought one of the "ineligibles" to Jesus. Then, Jesus would have had to say, "I'm sorry, brother, but God is teaching you something," or "God wants you to remain in this shape," "I'm sorry, brother, but you aren't eligible to be healed, because..." or, "I'm sorry, sister, but it is not my Father's will for you to be healed." or, "God is getting too much glory out of your sickness to heal you." But *that never happened* and *Jesus never said any of those things!* The reality is the **exact opposite.**

Had He said any of the above, we could correctly conclude, on the basis of that Scriptural precedent, that it was not God's will to heal everyone, and certainly not all who were willing to be healed. But, thankfully for us today, He did not. Therefore, all the Scriptural promises and examples of healing must stand as valid, if for no other reason than Jesus' own ministry. Thus, anyone who would minister to an ill person in the manner described above, telling them for instance that God wants them sick for a higher reason, is being inluenced by a spirit *other than the Holy Spirit.*

Neither did Jesus even have to pray about whether to heal someone or not. He knew perfectly well that the will of the Father was to heal everyone who sought healing, and so He simply healed everyone who came to Him!

The following excerpt is from an actual letter I received about twenty-five years ago from an eighty year old woman who wrote to thank me for praying for her and for the healing of her almost totally blind eyes. After we prayed God tripled the distance at which she could read. I told her that this was not only a sign of God's ability to heal, but also of His willingness, desire and intent to completely heal her specific condition. She wrote me a few weeks later to explain that she could not understand why her healing hadn't progressed more rapidly since the initial miracle.

When I read the concluding paragraph of her letter I realized that I had not communicated as much truth to her as I'd thought.

> *"So I, too, am now praying God to restore part of my sight, for reading has been a lifetime pleasure. I also have prayed "Thy will be done" and if for Your good reason, it is better for me to remain handicapped this way, I will accept it; glorifying God and not whining or complaining. I know God can, if He so deems it best."*

In her letter she hits several of the main blocks to healing:

"*Part*" implies His inability or unwillingness to heal completely.

"*Thy will be done*" assumes that healing may not be His will.

"*Your good reason*"indicates that God might prefer her to remain unhealed for His higher purposes.

"*If*" insults God.

"*To accept sickness*" as being from Him, also is an insult to Him.

I believe, if there were to be a choice, God would prefer that we doubted *His ability*, rather than *His desire* to heal us. "God is love" (I John 4:16)  It must grieve Him for us to doubt His intent.  What good earthly parent would not do all that *he or she could* to heal his or her child?

To use "if" would be like having your own child say to you, "Daddy, *if you love me,* will you feed me, and not let me starve to death?"  Such a question and doubt on his part would demonstrate that the child has no concept of a father's love for his own child.

### "Healing in Scripture Is Spiritual, Not Physical."

This is often used as an excuse by ministers who are reluctant to pray forcefully, or with faith, for someone's physical healing. The reality is that the will of God to heal your physical body is literally written in the self-healing design of your body. Had He not intended your body to be healed, He would not have designed your blood to clot, for instance. Because He did so, when you prick your finger, the wound quickly heals and you do not bleed to death. There are numerous other ways in which the body works to heal itself, including the generation of antibodies to combat infections and viruses, such as the flu.

Physical healing, therefore, is part of God's physical creation. How much greater this healing should be now that He has released His creative agent, the Holy Spirit, to His church.

* * *

If you have seen blocks in this chapter that you feel relate to you, you might start your prayer:

*Father, I am awed by Your love, goodness and ample provision for your people. Forgive me for accepting the world's view of You, and for doubting your goodness.*

* * *

"Our minds stagger at the implications of your goodness, and will to heal. How was healing provided to us?"

16

# Chapter 2

# God's Will Was Expressed in the Atonement

The atonement for all of mankind took place at the cross. Jesus' death on our behalf provided for our salvation, the healing of our innermost being. Could the same be true for our outermost being? As we will see, there is healing provided in the sacrifice of Jesus and there is healing proclaimed through Communion.

## Healing in the Atonement and Healing in Communion

There is a block to faith which occurs when we fail to discern the purpose of the Lord's Body. Clearly, the believer is expected to discern that the Lord's Body is meant to be whole.

Some in Paul's day did not, and some today still do not fully appreciate the symbolism of the sacred elements in the Communion observance, viewing it merely as a social function. Paul noted that wrong attitudes caused some to eat ahead of others and some to drink too heavily. Thus, they brought judgment upon themselves by eating unworthily. Jesus expands upon these truths in John Chapter 6, as does Paul in I Corinthians 10:16-17, 11:20-31, and 12:12-27.

By partaking of Communion as a member of His church, one becomes a member of the mystical, or spiritual *Body* of Christ. Just as it is offensive for us to consider the possibility of sickness indwelling the physical body of the Lord Jesus Christ as He walked the earth 2000 years ago, so should it be equally offensive to think of sickness residing now in His Personage in heaven. And as we join together as one body, as the Body of Christ through Communion, it should be equally offensive to think that sickness in our own bodies is somehow according to His will. *We are,* now, His Body on earth.

> *So we, being many, are one body in Christ, and every one members one of another.* Rom. 12:5

Sickness should no more reign in our bodies than it did in that of the Messiah. Jesus said, *Satan...hath nothing in me* (including sickness); the same should be true for Him, in us!

> *...the prince of this world cometh, and hath nothing in me.* John 14:30b

Many do not discern the body of Christ and its power to heal them. The reality is that Christians should not be continually searching for "a healing," but should rather be living in Divine health. With this thought in mind, there are three key truths to understand concerning His Body.

**1.) We must discern that the *breaking* of Jesus' physical body is observed through *the broken bread* of Communion, and thus healing was provided in the atonement**.

If we fail to grasp that truth, then we will not see the link between Communion and healing from Jesus. For further evidence of this, we look to what the Communion elements represent.

We know that the wine signifies the Blood, which was shed for the remission of our sins, and thus cleanses us and saves us. It also makes us *eligible* for healing. However, the Bread represents His body which was, for some specific meaning, broken for us. How was His body broken? Remember that "not a bone of Him was broken" in accordance with prophecy (John 19:33,36; Exo.12:46). Instead, His flesh was flayed from His back with the scourge which had bits of metal or glass attached to it, laying it open to the bone; and then His flesh was pierced by thorns and nails. This graphic picture is meant to emphasize that this part of His ordeal was not insignificant in the overall sacrifice and atonement. This breaking through beatings and lashings answers *how* His body was broken, now we must discern why.

It was at the whipping post during that flogging, that He willingly received the stripes on His flesh, that *paid* for our healing.

These thirty-nine stripes were one shy of a death penalty, to avoid double jeopardy, should a prisoner survive. The Romans were careful to give Jesus one less than forty stripes for that was legally considered a death penalty. Some physicians have maintained that there are thirty-nine categories of diseases.

Jesus Himself draws the distinction between the purposes of the shed Blood (the wine of Communion), and the purposes of His broken Body (the bread of Communion) in His own following explanations:

> *For this is **my blood** of the new testament, which is **shed for** many for **the remission of sins**.*
>
> Mat. 26:28

*And he took bread, and gave thanks, and **brake it**,
and gave unto them, saying, This is **my body** which is
given for you: this do in remembrance of me.*

Luke 22:19

The implication is that the **blood** alone was sufficient
for the remission of sins.  What then is the significance of
the **body**?  His blood was shed for our salvation, His body
was broken for our healing.

Isaiah provides confirmation of this solution to the
mystery of the presence of the "body" in Communion.

*But he was wounded for our transgressions, he was
bruised for our iniquities: the chastisement of our
peace was upon him; and **with his stripes we are
healed.*** Isa. 53:5

The *stripes* or *wounds* Isaiah is referring to are the
same as the *brokenness of the Lord's body* at the cross, as
presented in Communion! Through these stripes, or through
His broken body, "we are healed." Isaiah thus completes
the link between the marks on Christ's body, the "stripes,"
and the presence of the broken bread, or body, in Communion. Note that the Hebrew word Isaiah uses for "healing" is
*rapha'* and is defined as "to mend" and "to cure," very specific terms applied in the area of healing.

**2.) We must also discern or recognize the pres-
ence of Jesus within His collective, *spiritual* Body, the
Body of Christ now functioning on the earth as His
Church.**

If we fail to do so, then we will not be likely to either
summon the elders or to seek believing prayer from mem-

20

bers of that now present, Body of Christ. Today, it is Jesus in (or through) that Body who lays His hands upon the sick and makes them whole!

> *And these signs shall follow **them that believe**...they **shall lay hands on the sick**, and they shall recover.*
> Mark 16:17-18

### 3.) We must also understand that it is we – you and I – who are *that Body*.

Because we are members, we are eligible for His healing. In addition, since we are a part of the Body of Christ, then sickness should have no more legal right to exist in our bodies than it did to exist in the earthly, physical body of Jesus Christ!

### Calvary's Completed Work

To restate and underscore this vital truth: The blood was shed for our sins: the stripes upon His body were for our healing. To this fact, Jesus, Isaiah, Peter, Paul and Matthew testify.

He has borne our sicknesses in His broken body, and this is celebrated every time groups of believers come together for Communion. We should therefore be in agreement with His will, and be willing to fight the sickness through prayer. And we should acknowledge in confidence that this illness is absolutely outside His will for us. Every time we celebrate Communion, we proclaim healing!

### Has Jesus Already Borne Your Sickness?

As we shall see, Jesus *has* borne our sicknesses and diseases with the same completeness that He has borne our sins. Given this fact, we would be foolish indeed to attempt to bear them ourselves.

This becomes clear when we analyze the underlying language used in Peter and Isaiah. Notice the difference in verb tense:

> *But he was wounded for our transgressions, he was bruised for our iniquities: the chastisement of our peace was upon him; and with his stripes we __are__ healed.*
> Isa. 53:4-5

Isaiah looks forward through time to the Cross of Jesus and the work to be accomplished there, and he states: *we are* (or are to be) *healed.* Peter, likewise, quotes this same passage, but looks *back* upon it in light of the completed work of the Cross. As such, he puts the verse in the past tense, recognizing the fact that healing has already been provided at the cross.

> *Who his own self bare our sins in his own body on the tree, that we, being dead to sins, should live unto righteousness: by whose stripes ye __were__ healed.*
> 1 Pet. 2:24

A similar revelation occurs when we compare the words of Matthew to the core passage in Isaiah.

> *That it might be fulfilled which was spoken by Esaias the prophet, saying, **Himself took our infirmities, and bare our sicknesses**.*
> Mat. 8:17

The word used by Matthew and translated "bare" is the Greek word *bastazo (bas-tad'-zo)* meaning to "bear, carry, take up."

It is fascinating that this comes from a root word meaning "the foot" *basis, (bas'-ece)*. This is especially meaningful when we consider God's initial promise of a Savior in Genesis. Notice that it was prophetically stated in Eden that the area of the Seed to be bruised would be a part of the foot, and the nails which pierced His feet would also have bruised them.

> And I will put enmity between thee and the woman, and between thy seed and her **seed**; it shall bruise thy head, and thou shalt bruise **his heel**.     Gen. 3:15

The effect of His words is clear: Jesus took our infirmities, and bore our sicknesses. Matthew is quoting or referencing an Old Testament source, specifically, the words of Isaiah. By comparing Matthew's words in Greek to Isaiah's words in Hebrew, we will find an amazing parallel. Isaiah's words are:

> Surely he hath **borne** [nasa'] our griefs, and **carried** [cabal] our sorrows: yet we did esteem him stricken, smitten of God, and afflicted. But he was wounded for our transgressions, he was bruised for our iniquities: the chastisement of our peace was upon him; and with his stripes we are healed.     Isa. 53:4-5

Notice the key to unlock the message of healing in Matthew. Isaiah's "griefs" and "sorrows" are the same as Matthew's "infirmities" and "sicknesses!" The Messiah, through bearing our spiritual woes on the cross has specifically addressed our physical sickness as well. And as Isaiah completes this thought, by His stripes or broken body, we are healed.

The word used by Isaiah rendered "borne" is nasa' (naw-saw'). It means to lift, as well as to suffer, to bear (-er, up), to carry (away), to spare, to take (away, up). He

23

used a different Hebrew word for "carried," *cabal*, (*saw-bal'*) which also means to carry, or bear, burden. Jesus *took up, suffered because of,* and *carried away* our sickness, along with our sin.

Furthermore, the word *cabal* is used again in the same chapter of Isaiah, in a fascinating way.

*He shall see of the travail of his soul, and shall be satisfied: by his knowledge shall my righteous servant justify many; for he shall **bear** [cabal] their iniquities.*                                    Isa. 53:11

Precisely the same word is used in Scripture to describe the Suffering Servant's "carrying away" of our iniquities (in verse 53:11) that is used to describe His "carrying away" of our sicknesses (in verse 53:4)! The Spirit wants us to understand that what applies to our sins also applies to our sickness. If He has borne our sins, then He has, with equal totality, borne our sicknesses. And, if He has borne our sickness on the cross at Calvary, there is absolutely no reason for us to continue to carry our own sickness. It is no longer our sickness, He has paid the price for it; it belongs to Him - get your hands off *His* sickness!

Likewise, the Son of God was sent to earth in order to destroy the works of the devil. What actions did Jesus take that would constitute destroying Satan's work? He opened the doorway of salvation, he cast out demons, and **he healed the sick**.

*...For this purpose the Son of God was manifested, that he **might destroy the works of the devil**.*
1 John 3:8

And this purpose was prophesied well before Jesus came to earth, as in Isaiah above, and also in Malachi.

*But for you who revere my name, the sun of righteous-*
*ness will rise with healing in its wings.*　　Mal. 4:2

## Knowing Jesus, the Son,
## As a Loving Heavenly Father

Many individuals do not recognize Jesus to be a Loving Heavenly Father. One of the titles for the Messiah, given by Isaiah was,

*For unto us a child is born, unto us a son is given:*
*and the government shall be upon his shoulder: and*
*his name shall be called Wonderful, Counsellor, The*
*mighty God, The everlasting **Father**, The Prince of*
*Peace.*　　Isa.  9:6

Jesus Himself told Philip,

*...he that hath seen me hath seen **the Father**; and how*
*sayest thou then, Show us the Father? Believest thou*
*not that I am in the Father, and the Father in me?*
　　John 14:9b-10a

Jesus' own loving Heavenly Father said of Himself,

*For I know the thoughts that I think toward you, saith*
*the LORD, thoughts of peace, and not of evil, to give*
*you an expected end.*　　Jer. 29:11

Consider also that Jesus invited us to ask of Him:

*Hitherto have ye asked nothing in my name: ask, and*
*ye shall receive, that your joy may be full.*
　　John 16:24

Obviously, Jesus is a loving Father who is concerned about our needs, and wants us to ask of Him, in order that He might grant us what we ask. I find it absolutely amazing, that the God of the Universe not only allows us to ask but **desires us to ask**, so that He might do great things for us, and make our joy complete!

God wishes that you might be filled with joy – what a blessed thought! Yet, that is exactly what we, as good, loving earthly fathers desire for our own little children.

With that thought in mind, consider one of my favorite illustrations, which I use to encourage the faith of those needing healing.

### *The Bicycle Illustrations*

When a father promises his child that he will buy him a bicycle, the child accepts his father's promise. This is in spite of the fact that the child knows nothing about his father's bank balance, or actual capacity to perform his word. The child *trusts*, simply because he *loves* his father and *believes* he has told him the truth. (*Whosoever shall not receive the kingdom of God as a little child shall in no wise enter therein.* Luke 18:17)

Let's take this illustration a little further. Let's assume that two eight-year olds, one is my son and the other is yours, come to you and ask, politely, for you to buy them a bicycle. For which of the two are you more likely to buy a bicycle, your son or mine? I would suggest it would be your son, of course. But why? Because he is your own son, and you have a commitment to him.

Next, let's put ourselves in the position of the two boys: which will have the greater expectancy (or more faith) of actually receiving a bike? Again, it is your son, because he knows you and your love for him. He has a relationship with you, and trusts you.

26

Now we alter our example again: now it is two individuals approaching God, this time not merely for a bike, but for something far more important – healing: you as a son of God and another man who is a stranger. Who will have the greater faith or expectancy of receiving a healing? Naturally, you as a son of God. Why? Because you have a basis for approach, a relationship. You are in a blood relationship with Him, as His beloved adopted son. You have an inheritance to claim, through His word.

## Conclusion of The Matter
### Countering Erroneous Teaching On Healing

As discussed before, there are seeds that have been planted in our minds and souls that war against our faith regarding healing, and discourage us from seeking the Lord's love and power. More often than not, these are planted by those who are themselves blinded to the power of God, and the modern day ministry of Jesus Christ. A few of these "seeds" are presented below.

### "Help, I Think God Wants Me Dead"

I suspect every patient who is told that he is terminally ill feels as if the above were true. After all, we reason, if God didn't want me dead, I wouldn't have this terminal illness.

First, we must recognize the fact that if God wanted you to be dead, you would already *be dead!* That thought always gave me comfort in the days when I was under a death sentence with cancer. Second, if you really believe that God wants you dead, why are you resisting death by seeking medical help? Third, what role does the devil play, who was called a "murderer from the beginning" (John 8:44)?

## "God Has Given Me this Sickness
## to Teach Me Something."

Our God is a perfect communicator. If this idea were correct, and He gave sickness to teach people things, how do we explain all the hospitals full of people who can't get the message! This logic makes God look like a pretty *poor communicator*. God didn't make His disciples sick in order to teach them something, Rather, He told them parables, and demonstrated to them His power!

## "God Has Some Higher Purpose
## in My Being Sick or Afflicted."

That thinking always makes you feel a little better and more willing to accept your affliction. I remember saying to myself one night back in 1970, "Well God must have some higher purpose in giving me cancer and having me die at age thirty-two." Of course I was wrong. God's "higher purpose" was for me to be healed and to proclaim His power to save and heal others!

## "God Has Given Me this Sickness
## to Slow Me down"

That's another obvious rationalization. The height of the ridiculousness of this rationalization is to be seen in the cases of two local pastors, who both had mental breakdowns, and were placed in psychiatric wards. The explanation that I heard from the people in their churches was that these men had their mental breakdowns in order to slow them down, and so that they could witness to the people in the psychiatric wards. Blatantly foolish, and ludicrous! Anyone from the outside looking at that rationally can see the error of it. Did Jesus have to contract leprosy to heal lepers? Of course not.

* * *

If  you have seen blocks in this chapter that you feel relate to you, you might start your prayer:

*Lord Jesus, we thank You for Your completed work upon the cross, whereby You  paid the price in full for all our sins.  And we thank You for puchasing our healing with Your stripes.  Grant us the wisdom and grace to walk in the fullness of Your completed work.*

* * *

If indeed, God wants me well and did not give me my condition, where could it have come from?

# Chapter 3

# Satan's Will Regarding Healing

## Not Knowing The True Source of Sickness

As I have indicated, my biggest problem during my terminal illness thirty years ago was that I assumed God to be the source of my cancer. I did not realize that there could be another source.

### Who Caused Your Sickness?

What is the true source of your sickness? Actually a better question is, *"Who* is the source of your sickness?" Does the loving God, who created you, want you to be sick? Could the same God described as love and light, also be hate and darkness? Is the same God who sent His Son to die for you, a tormentor and murderer?

*God is love*                                        1 John 4:16

*God is light, and in him is no darkness at all.*
                                                      1 John 1:5

It cannot be so. This idea that God causes sickness is, in fact, one of Satan's most commonly believed lies. Just as it was Satan who smote Job with illness (Job 2:7- See Chapter Eight) so it is also Satan who has smitten you.

### Not Knowing *Satan* to be the Source of Sickness

It is essential for our faith that we know where our sickness originates, for if we believe it to be from God, we cannot effectively resist it. There is absolutely no doubt, as far as Scripture is concerned, as to who the true source of death and disease actually is. A contrast is seen between the ministries of Jesus and Satan in John 10.

> *The thief cometh not, but for to steal, and to kill, and to destroy: I am come that they might have life, and that they might have it more abundantly.*   John 10:10

Jesus came that we might have life: Satan's goal is death for all those born of God. It is Satan, and not God, who is the author of sickness, disease, and premature death. Permit me to offer Scriptural proof of the Satanic source of sickness: there are at least **eight** witnesses to Satan as the source of sickness...

## The First Witness

Jesus is the first witness. He testified that Satan *was a murderer from the beginning* (John 8:44). And in Luke 13, He identified Satan, specifically, as the one who was responsible for a woman being bowed over in a crippling bondage of infirmity.

This later passage was quickened to me in 1970 when I was searching for healing truths, while dying of cancer. It was really an eye-opener for me, when I saw that Jesus Himself identified the *specific cause* of that particular woman's problem as Satan! He didn't say, "*God* gave her that affliction," as I would have expected, based upon what I had been taught. Nor, did Jesus say that God did such things for "some higher purpose."

> *And ought not this woman, being a daughter of Abraham, whom **Satan hath bound**, lo, these eigh-*

*teen years, be loosed from this bond on the sabbath*
*day?*                                          Luke 13:16

## The Second Witness

David is the second witness. He identifies Satan as the Destroyer, and as the source of his own affliction.

*...by the word of thy lips I have kept me from the*
*paths of **the destroyer**.*                    Psa. 17:4

*An **evil disease**,* [a thing of Belial, or Satan)] *say they,*
*cleaveth fast unto him: and now that he lieth he shall*
*rise up no more.*                              Psa. 41:8

## The Third Witness

Malachi, in his third chapter, says that if we are faithful to God with our tithes and offerings, He will rebuke *the Devourer* for our sakes. The Devourer is the one who would eat us up, and the one who would destroy us physically or in any other way that he could. And that being is Satan.

## The Fourth Witness

Paul also recognizes that Satan is the Destroyer of human flesh. In 1st Corinthians he speaks of a sinning Brother, who refused to cease from his transgressions. Paul surrenders this man over to Satan, who is described as the one responsible for the "destruction of the flesh."

*To deliver such an one unto Satan for the **destruction***
***of the flesh**...*                            1 Cor. 5:5a

## The Fifth Witness

Peter also sees Satan as the Devourer, and as the source of affliction. He contrasts him with Jesus, who is the source of "healing" for "all that were oppressed by the Devil." The devil's oppression is countered by the Messiah's healing ministry!

> *Be sober, be vigilant; because your adversary the **devil**, as a roaring lion, walketh about, seeking whom he may **devour**: Whom resist stedfast in the faith, knowing that the same **afflictions** are accomplished in your brethren that are in the world.*
>
> 1 Pet. 5:8-9

> *How God anointed Jesus of Nazareth with the Holy Ghost and with power: who went about doing good, and **healing** **all that were oppressed of the devil**; for God was with him.*
>
> Acts 10:38

## The Sixth Witness

John states that the purpose for which Jesus came into the world was to *undo*, or to *destroy*, the works of the Devil.

> *For this purpose the Son of God was manifested, that he might destroy **the works of the devil**.*
>
> 1 John 3:8

And so we ask, what did Jesus do? He healed the sick, cast out demons, raised the dead, and opened the doorway of salvation. Jesus openly displayed His power by destroying Satan's destructive work on the bodies and souls of men, through healings and salvation. **The afflictions of the body and soul were thus the "works of the Devil."** Every time that Jesus healed a body or cast out a demon, He was demonstrating the superiority of the Kingdom of God over the kingdom of darkness.

## The Seventh Witness

The Holy Spirit is our seventh witness, when he identifies Satan as the source of man's afflictions. He does so as the Source of inspiration of Job, a work considered to be the oldest book of the Bible.

*So went **Satan** forth from the presence of the LORD, and **smote Job** with sore boils from the sole of his foot unto his crown.*                               Job 2:7

And He refers to all of Job's afflictions as being his "captivity."

*And the LORD turned **the captivity** of Job, when he prayed for his friends: also the LORD gave Job twice as much as he had before.*                    Job 42:10

Satan is the "strong man" described by Jesus in His parable.

*But if I with the finger of God cast out devils, no doubt the kingdom of God is come upon you. When a **strong man** armed keepeth his palace, his goods are in peace: But when **a stronger** than he shall come upon him, and overcome him, he taketh from him all his armour wherein he trusted, and divideth his spoils.*
                                Luke 11:20-22

Satan is thus presented to be the same one who has taken men "captive by him at *his* will" (2 Tim. 2:26). The good news is that Jesus is the **Stronger Man**, who has overcome him, casting out devils with "the finger of God" (or, "the Spirit of God" - Mat. 12:28), and thus dividing his spoils; that is, "setting his captives free" (Luke 4:18).

## The Eighth Witness

The final witness is **God** the Father, who also identifies disease as *evil*. Since God is good, and He declared everything that He created to be very "good" (Gen. 1:31), something "evil" by definition must be a work of the Devil.

> *And the LORD will take away from thee all sickness, and will put none of the **evil diseases** of Egypt.*
>
> Deut. 7:15a

Along those lines, Jesus proclaimed that everything He did was in accordance with the will of the Father. And that includes His dynamic, miraculous healing ministry!

In addition, the **Holy Spirit** directed **Paul** to record the revelation that premature death, which is our enemy, has been controlled by Satan.

> *Forasmuch then as the children are partakers of flesh and blood, he also himself likewise took part of the same; that through death he might destroy him that had the **power of death**, that is, the devil; And deliver them who through fear of death were all their lifetime subject to bondage.*
>
> Heb. 2:14-15

> *The last **enemy** that shall be destroyed is death.*
>
> 1 Cor. 15:26

Having exposed the foundation of all sickness as Satan, we may take the next step in exposing the power behind this evil strongman. For instance, one might assume that "Since I am not healed...."

## "Satan Must Have a Hold on Me."

This is an interesting issue: how might Satan obtain or maintain a hold on an individual? I believe there are several ways, and I have listed seven following:

1.) A person can chose to remain in Satan's power by **rejecting Jesus** and His offer of salvation. To not accept Jesus is to choose to remain in the darkness of Satan's kingdom, and under the influence of the *evil strongman*. And to reject salvation is to reject the atoning blood sacrifice of Jesus Christ to save.

> *He (Satan) hath blinded their eyes, and hardened their heart; that they should not see with their eyes, nor understand with their heart, and be converted, and I should heal them.* John 12:40

To reject salvation is to also reject the power of the broken body of Jesus to heal, and all the healing promises written throughout the Old and New Testaments.

2.) A person can give Satan a *place,* or *legal right,* to remain within through **harboring anger**:

> *Be ye angry, and sin not: let not the sun go down upon your wrath: Neither **give place to the devil**.* Eph. 4:26-27

3.) A person can give Satan a *place,* or *legal right,* to remain through **unforgiveness**. Note that the tormentors mentioned below are demonic agents of Satan.

> *And his lord was wroth, and delivered him to the tormentors, till he should pay all that was due unto him. So likewise shall my heavenly Father do also unto you, if ye **from your hearts forgive not** every one his brother their trespasses.* Mat. 18:35

4.) The individual believer who has not consciously repented of his sins and sought forgiveness for himself may also leave spiritual doors open, unknowingly. **Refusing to repent, confess or renounce past involvement with the enemy** is also to reject the need for forgiveness for sins. Refusing the cleansing blood of Jesus is to refuse to walk in daily forgiveness and to repent whenever needed.

*But if we walk in the light, as he is in the light, we have fellowship one with another, and the **blood of Jesus** Christ his Son **cleanseth us from all sin**. If we confess our sins, he is faithful and just to forgive us our sins, and to cleanse us from all unrighteousness.*
1 John 1:7,9

*We know that whosoever is born of God sinneth not; but he that is begotten of God keepeth himself, and that **wicked one toucheth him not**.*          John 5:18

5.) Satan may have a claim if there **is a specific tie to the occult** in the person's past, a tie which has not been properly addressed and broken. Unfortunately, even for born again believers, past involvement with the occult may need to be specifically dealt with, through repentance and deliverance, unless this was sovereignly taken care of at the moment of salvation.

This claim may be based upon direct involvement in the occult, or idolatry, false religion, false worship, and false doctrines (such as reincarnation, which denies the need for a Savior). Certainly any continued access to these spiritually dangerous practices will mean trouble for the believer. God has called His people to come out of worldliness and to be separated unto Him. And this is in part for our own protection!

*And what agreement hath the temple of God with idols? for ye are the temple of the living God; as God hath said, I will dwell in them, and walk in them; and I will be their God, and they shall be my people. Wherefore come out from among them, and be ye separate, saith the Lord, and touch not the unclean thing; and I will receive you*          2 Cor. 6:16-17

6.) Another cause is if the **person has been disobedient to God**. An example would be Moses, for whose body Satan apparently thought he had a claim, based upon Moses' disobedience (which only resulted in his loss of an earthly blessing, not an eternal separation from God. Otherwise Michael would not have been fighting for him after his death).

*Yet Michael the archangel, when contending with the devil he disputed about the body of Moses, durst not bring against him a railing accusation, but said, The Lord rebuke thee.*         Jude 1:9

7.) The person **has refused to receive deliverance from demonic bondages**. When an individual knows that he is in bondage, but refuses to seek deliverance, he is *choosing* to remain in Satan's power.

Each of the individuals in the above seven categories is, in essence, still on Satan's turf, still eligible to be afflicted, and to be harassed and tormented either by him or by his agents. Having said all this, *sometimes Satan afflicts God's servants in an attempt to frustrate their service and efforts for the kingdom.* There is a great need for intercession on behalf of people who walk on the "front lines" of battle. As an uplifting thought, have you ever thought that your sickness may be related to the fact that you hold great promise for the kingdom of God, and the devil is fighting mad – attempting to prevent you from attaining your proper position? In this sense, we hold close the following promise: Jesus Himself intercedes on our behalf 24 hours a day, 7 days a week.

> *Who is he that condemneth? It is Christ that died, yea rather, that is risen again, who is even at the right hand of God, who also maketh intercession for us.*
>
> Rom. 8:34

## Can Satan Heal?

Yes, if it is to his advantage. **He will often exchange a lesser sickness for a worse one.** There are numerous examples of counterfeit healing techniques in the New Age world of holistic healing. Often, when receiving a gift from the satanic kingdom, a far greater bondage is part of the exchange...

## Exchange: Epilepsy for a Broken Arm

We know of a young boy who was hit by a car, and the bones in his right arm were splintered beyond repair. His parents took him to a Christian Science practitioner, who read to him throughout the night. The following day they could not find a trace of a break in his arm. But to this day that boy is plagued with epilepsy, a condition that was totally absent prior.

There is a principle which we (and others) have observed over the years, which is that when someone goes to a source other than Jesus Christ for a healing, there is often an exchange that takes place. In this boy's case, in place of the broken arm, Satan apparently gave him epilepsy. If we accept the fact that Satan is the source of sicknesses, disease and death, then it is obvious that he is the one who puts sicknesses on people and, if it should suit his purposes, he can also remove a sickness. Because he is inherently evil, he cannot actually carry out a righteous act, and therefore he merely replaces the former condition with what usually proves to be a worse form of affliction.

As a result of Satan getting a foothold within the family of that boy, through their seeking "alternative healing," to this day (nearly fifty years later) his entire family has remained antagonistic towards the gospel, in spite of witnessing powerful demonstrations of God's love and power.

## Satan Wields the Weapon of Sickness

Satan's primary weapons are ignorance and fear. However, sicknesses or temporary afflictions against the people of God  also seem to be favorite weapons in Satan's arsenal.  His attempts to prevent people from getting to places where they can receive healing or deliverance have already been mentioned.  In addition, he will afflict individuals in an attempt to prevent them from moving deeper into the things of God, such as receiving salvation, the Baptism with the Holy Spirit, from being used as an instrument by God in making healing or deliverance available.  As an example, I have never been sicker in my life than I was when, as a cancer patient, I first attended a Kathryn Kuhlman meeting.

To illustrate the latter point above, I hosted one of the first deliverance conferences held in St. Louis in 1972.  A group of us invited a nationally known minister, who agreed to come and teach a series of meetings. The first night of the conference, that minster was hit with a digestive upset. He had his wife relay a message for me to go on to the church and start the meeting, while they waged spiritual warfare for him to be able to make the meeting.

With knee-knocking faith, I  faced a crowd of nearly a thousand people and announced that the speaker would be there shortly.  He managed to arrive before the worship concluded, and we had a glorious meeting that greatly influenced our area. In similar fashion I have sometimes been hit when attempting to get to various terminally ill patients. Satan always over-plays his hand, and we eventually catch on to his schemes. We have come to discover a principle: that *the greater the opposition, the greater the potential blessing God has in store.*

How can this be? Can Satan read God's mind? No he certainly cannot. However, I do believe that Satan can observe increased angelic activity in an area where God is about to move mightily. And so, fiend that he is, he dispenses his troops of demonic agents, his *aggelos,* in an attempt to frustrate the purposes of God, whatever they might be. Because he is intelligent enough to know that God is working to bring about good, he seeks to oppose those eforts with evil.

## Recognize That Every Objection To Healing Is Demonically Inspired.

No matter how logical the argument is, or how "holy" the source seems to be, this bold statement remains as true today as it did 2000 years ago. Satan is behind every "anti-healing" argument. He is behind every denial that Jesus is Lord of Lord and King of Kings, and every denial that Jesus is all that God said that He is. We should not be surprised that Satan is, therefore, also behind the denial of Jesus' claim that He is the "God that Healeth Thee."

*I have set before you life and death, blessing and cursing: therefore choose life, that both thou and thy seed may live:*    Deut. 30:19

Although Satan is the root cause of all sickness, disease and premature death, he is aided in his work by a myriad of agents otherwise known as evil spirits or demons.

## Not Knowing Demons
## Are Involved in Affliction

It is abundantly clear in Scripture that demonic activity is involved in many kinds of sickness. The Bible specifically mentions deaf and dumb spirits, spirits of blindness, spirits of infirmity, in addition to evil, foul, seducing, and unclean spirits. Jesus, by His actions and His words, declared evil spirits, or demons, to be the source of many afflictions.

*Then was brought unto him one possessed with a **devil**, blind, and dumb: and he healed him, insomuch that the blind and dumb both spake and saw.*
Mat. 12:22

*And, behold, there was a woman which had a **spirit of infirmity** eighteen years, and was bowed together, and could in no wise lift up herself.* Luke 13:11

Note that, in the Gospels, **Jesus is never recorded as having *prayed* for healing.** Rather, He simply confidently *commanded* the sick to be well, the deaf to hear, and the blind to see. So it is today, we are *to command* Satan and his forces to leave the bodies of the sick (including our own). Rarely, is this done in our churches, and thus rarely do we see dramatic healings today in the church. And we know that it is not God who has changed!

Thus, we can confidently assert:

## Sickness is the Will of Satan;
## It is Not God's will for His people.

Sometimes, when a condition does not respond to prayer, or prayer *plus* will power, or even prayer *plus* will power *plus* fasting, then perhaps there is at the root a block

43

that is demonic. Since we have seen Satan to be the basic cause of all sickness, it is not illogical that demons, doing his bidding, may be seeking to prevent a healing. Here is what I discovered in the case of Gloria.

## Gloria and a Demon of Hate

One evening, I was invited to speak in a private home to a group of about a dozen middle-aged women. After I gave my testimony, I offered prayer for healing and each of the women present was apparently healed of a variety of conditions. All the pain left each one as I held their feet, and then prayed for them.

During the prayer time, one young woman had her back healed after she overcame an unforgiveness block. She forgave the people who had caused the auto accident, which had injured her. She came back a little later, after watching other people get healed, and said,

"Bill, what do you think the Lord can do about this?" And she attempted to raise her right arm, halting it in a not fully horizontal position.

I replied, "What do you have, a frozen shoulder?"

She said, "Yeah."

I asked, "How long have you had that?"

She said, "Well I guess it's from the same accident that we prayed for before when my back was healed."

I asked, "Why didn't you have me pray for the shoulder when we prayed earlier?"

"I guess, I just forgot about it, because I've lived with it for so long."

"Well, we can pray for it right now."

Then she asked, "Are you going to anoint me again, and shall I sit back in the 'prayer chair'?"

"No," I responded, "you've already been anointed, we'll just trust that same healing anointing is still valid for you." Then, facing her, I put my hands on her shoulder and began to pray gently for her. As soon as I did, she began to jerk and twitch.

After a minute she opened one eye and said, "Bill, I'm having a reaction to your prayer."

I replied, "I don't think it's *you* that's reacting to my prayer. I think it's something within you, and we're just going to treat that 'thing' as if it's a demon – we're going to command that thing to come out."

She said simply, "Okay."

As she closed her eyes, I continued to pray, and commanded whatever the thing was that was causing her to jerk and twitch to manifest itself, to name itself, and to come out of her. Almost immediately, a deep, gruff male voice from within her boomed out, "HATRED," so loud that the windows in the little house rattled!

I then told her, "Okay, command "Hatred" to leave you."

She said, "In the Name of Jesus, you spirit of Hatred – get out of me!"

Next, she began to rejoice, "Praise God, I felt that thing go..." and she raised both her arms upward in praise to the Lord. Then glancing down at her right shoulder, she realized that she had been healed, and that her frozen shoulder was completely free. She exclaimed, "Look at that – my arm is healed! I wouldn't have believed that I had an evil spirit, but I felt that 'thing' go."

Recognize this simple fact: we could have prayed ourselves blue in the face over that young woman, trying to get her stiff shoulder healed, but until the root problem of hatred was confronted, and the spirit of Hatred cast out, there was a block to her complete healing.

### "I Refuse to Believe That *I* Could Have a Demon!"

This is another form of limiting God. Often man limits

God by the traditions in which he believes. For example: "I believe God can heal me anyway he wants to, BUT I refuse to believe in the possibility that I could have a demon, or need deliverance." Or, some might profess, "My denomination teaches that I, as a Christian, cannot possibly have a demon."

Remember all those Jesus healed that were afflicted with spirits of infirmity. What would that theology have done for Gloria?[1]

## "Must I Be Baptised with the Holy Spirit to Be Healed?"

No, of coure you do not need to be. (None of those whom Jesus healed in Person were.) However, I would strongly suggest that you seek the Baptism, especially if you are battling for you health. You apparently need more power, and we all need all the power of the Holy Spirit we can obtain. Jesus promised those who receive it would also receive power. (Acts 1:8) See Appendix.

* * *

If you have seen blocks in this chapter that you feel relate to you, you might start your prayer:

*Father, forgive me for not recognizing the Scripturally obvious truth that Satan is the source of all evil, including all forms of disease. Forgive me also, if I have consciously or unconciously blamed you for my own sickness, or that of others, and continue to reveal your truth to my heart."*

[1] For those wishing more information about demons, and their functioning, as well as many more possible demonic blocks to healing, we suggest the author's *Power for Deliverance* series. Also see the listing of healings in the Appendix.

A man who is perfectly well can still lay down on the inside and die, as we will see illustrated in Chapter Nine. **We do have a part to play in the decision whether to live or to die.**

Man was created with a strong will to live, but there are also certain decisions which he must make.

"I now recognize that God wants me well, and Satan wants me sick, but what must *I* do?"

# Chapter 4

# "How Important Is the Will of Man in Healing?"

That man has a role in his own fate is nothing new. We know that our salvation is based on a decision of the will, to either accept or deny Jesus as our Lord and Savior. In the process, we repent of our sins and surrender our old lives to become new creations. This requires a decision of the human will.

We also know that prayer is a requisite part of our lives as Christians. Jesus Himself told us to pray, or to set our wills toward prayer, and with good reason. There is power in prayer, and when we ask the Lord for help or assistance through prayer, He hears us and responds. A few verses back this up:

> *What things soever ye desire, when ye pray, believe that ye receive them, and ye shall have them.*
>
> Mark 11:24

> *The effectual fervent prayer of a righteous man availeth much* (or, "is powerful"!)      James 5:16

Prayer is the manifestation of our innermost needs and desires, in other words – our will. And it takes an act of will in order to pray. Yet through our prayers, things happen in the physical, which otherwise would not have happened. This is incredible power placed in the hands of the children of God.

Many, though, are surprised to learn that man has a part to play in his own healing. Apparently, they expect God to do everything necessary, on His own. The reality is that a lack of action is harmful; it does not allow a person's will to be fully asserted, and for the power of God to be made manifest.

It is important to point out, as well, that God will not heal *against* the will of the individual (candidate). This is why we cannot simply go and empty the hospitals, as unbelievers often challenge us to do; "If Jesus really wants to heal everyone." He *does* want to heal everyone, just as He wants all to be saved, but He will not force salvation upon the unwilling, either. A person's will in the matter plays a hugely important role.

Why are some not willing? As we will learn, some people aren't sure if they want to be well.

## The Will of the Individual

God designed your body to be self-healing, and placed within your soul a strong will for self-preservation. Thus, you were designed well, to be well. God has done His part, now it is up to us to do our part, and to make proper decisions in order to seek healing if needed, or to maintain our health.

The first thing one must do to become an eligible candidate for God's healing power is to accept Jesus as Lord and Savior. As noted in Chapter 2, the same promises made by the Messiah to remove our sins apply to our sicknesses as well; He bore our sins and He bore our sicknesses through the atoning sacrifice at the cross.

Secondly, a person needs to have a right attitude, a will to be healed. In the early days of our ministry, one of the men attending our Thursday night meetings commented,

"I have seen you fence with people for half an hour to get them to the point that you could pray for them." Actually, I think he missed the point. I was verbally fencing with them in order to get *them* to the point of accepting God's love for what it really is, and thus being eligible for the blessing of a touch of His healing power. In those cases, a human will had to be changed.

Many people come to God with wrong attitudes towards Him, and with a misunderstanding of the healing process. Some, for instance, come unrepentant, and some come almost daring Him to heal them. Others come haughtily, demanding or pridefully expecting His healing, basing their approach to Him on how good they have been, rather than coming to Him humbly and relying upon *His* goodness.

### Not Fulfilling Our Own Role.

*Verily, verily, I say unto you, He that believeth on me, the works that I do shall he do also;* ***and greater works than these shall he do****; because I go unto my Father.*
John 14:12

One who relies upon someone else to have faith is not going to recognize their own role: to pray, to continue to pray, to actively seek healing, or to seek others to pray for them. And if they fail to grasp the truth that the Spirit came to enable *men* to do "greater works" as Jesus said, then they are not going to submit themselves to men in anticipation of receiving healing.

We must fulfill our role in the pursuit of healing through first building our faith and second, by calling on others in the Church to do great works on our behalf, through the power and the might of the Holy Spirit.

## Believing That Because God is Sovereign, He Does not Need Us to Do Anything.

Since mankind inherently seeks the easiest route, the above belief is an oft repeated rationale for inaction. Of course, God did not need our input at creation. However, with regard to our own healings, we have been given free wills, and these He will not violate. The same is true, after all, for our salvation.

Too many expect a magic wand of healing to be waved over them, not realizing that a battle is being waged in the spiritual realm. Our answer for the battle set before us is prayer.

*And he spake a parable unto them to this end, that men **ought always to pray**, and not to faint*
Luke 18:1

*And I say unto you, Ask, and it shall be given you; seek, and ye shall find; knock, and it shall be opened unto you.*
Luke 11:9

The tense employed indicates that this refers to *ongoing, continuous* action. In other words "ask, and keep on asking," "seek, and keep on seeking," "knock, and keep on knocking"... and you shall receive.

Satan loves to do anything he can to prevent us from asking the Lord for our needs. If we lack knowledge, we need to learn. Likewise, if we doubt the Lord's will to heal, we need to come to believe that Jesus is alive and well and still able to heal today. If we aren't aware of that, then we're not going to have the faith to ask, and we're not going to be able to ask in faith. He responds to our requests, and to our cries:

*Then they **cry unto the LORD** in their trouble, and he saveth them out of their distresses. He sent his word, and healed them, and delivered them from their destructions.* Psa. 107:19-20

Consider also that Jesus encourages us to ask of Him:

*Hitherto have ye asked nothing in my name: ask, and ye shall receive, that your joy may be full.*
John 16:24

## Can Man Indeed Resist God's Healing Power?

There were two cases which I encountered in the first year of my ministry, that were particularly enlightening with regard to man's role in his own healing.

### Case 1: A Decision *Not to Receive* Healing

The first occurred one night when we were praying for healing in a private home. We had prayed for the healing of every person with a need, when the young minister present suggested, "Why don't you pray for my wife? She has a bad back."

We agreed, and as I held her feet the short leg began to move out, but then stopped. It seemed to refuse to budge, until finally the young minister joined us in prayer and it very begrudgingly finished moving out.

A week later in the privacy of his study, he asked, "Bill, would you like to know why my wife's leg wouldn't move last week, when you prayed for her?"

I said, "I sure would." At that time, I had never encountered a leg that had started to move out, and then stopped moving.

He explained, "My wife is a church organist, and she was afraid that if her leg were to be lengthened, she would no longer be able to play the floor keyboard of the organ,

53

and so *she made a decision* not to let her leg move."

I realize this is offensive theology for most of us. Man cannot limit God, only God can limit God. However, **God has voluntarily limited Himself to work within the framework of our freewill.** God will not heal individuals against their wills. **We have to *want* to be healed**, which is why Jesus often asked afflicted individuals what they wanted Him to do for them!

God will not heal you against your will, any more than He will save you against your will. **Your will is involved in everything you receive from God.**

As we have seen, it's possible for man to limit God: to not have enough faith, or to have our faith limited or restricted until God to lovingly stretches it for us. It is important to note that praying for God to increase our faith is often necessary in difficult situations.

The second case involves our willingness to receive from God according to His method. Some people are unwilling to be healed God's way; to let God be sovereign. Usually this is a result of pride. For example, Jesus used spit and mud in one instance to restore sight to a blind person. It is not very glamorous to have spit and mud dribbling down your cheeks. Are you willing to be healed by Jesus His way? Using His methods? His timing?

The method of His choosing might not be as dignified as going in a suit and tie to a doctor's office, and then paying for his services. Mud isn't dignified; spit isn't dignified, but the results were amazing. So it's important to be flexible, to allow God to be God, to allow God to be sovereign.

### Case 2:  Healing, but Not *That* Way!

A little over thirty years ago, my wife Sue and I were invited to speak in a home. At the end of the meeting, after we had given our testimony, we prayed for healing as we usually do so, and several people were healed. Finally our hostess said, "Well maybe I ought to have you pray for me."

I asked, "What do you need?"

She replied, "I had polio as a child, and I can play tennis, but not very well. My one leg is half the size of the other leg, in diameter, and it's also shorter."

So we prayed for her. I usually have people sit in a chair as I kneel in front of them and hold their outstretched feet. This way I can compare the length of the legs and watch God do His miraculous work! Accordingly, I held both her feet, and as I did, the withered leg began to vibrate like a tuning fork.

She said, "I know *I'm not* doing that, and I know that *you're not* doing that."

When we were through, the legs were the same length! However, there was no visible difference in the size of the legs. As such, she still seemed rather skeptical.

Shortly thereafter she moved to Florida, and about a year later I received a letter of apology from her, in which she wrote, "I think I was completely healed that night, or my healing certainly began that night. But," she added, "I had *a **mental block against it***, because I thought the 'holding of feet' was just a parlor game. It wasn't until I got down here to Florida and encountered a couple of other groups of sincere Christians, who did the same sort of thing, that I began to see the validity of the ministry."

She continued, "I didn't have anyone else pray for me, but my mind suddenly accepted the fact that this was valid, and it was from God. Today my leg is exactly the same size as my other leg!"

As a result of her prejudice, there was a negative faith block there, until God lovingly removed it.

Doubt and unbelief can be brought to bear upon you,

as a candidate for healing, from within. In addition, doubt can come from onlookers and scoffers, or even from those attempting to minister to you. In Matthew 13, when Jesus returned to His own home, we read:

*And they were offended in him. But Jesus said unto them, A prophet is not without honour, save in his own country, and in his own house. And he did not many mighty works there **because of their unbelief**.*

Mat. 13:57-58

Notice that Jesus *couldn't* heal – because of their unbelief. The onlookers' unbelief (community unbelief) *blocked* Jesus' power to heal those in need. This is offensive to our Christian theology, yet the Word declares it to be so...**man's will set against healing can block healing!** (As the two previous cases illustrate.)

### Are You a Victim of Negative Faith?

Clearly, there are negative faith factors. Mark amplifies upon the above passage from Matthew.

*Is not this the carpenter, the son of Mary, the brother of James, and Joses, and of Juda, and Simon? and are not his sisters here with us? And they were offended at him. But Jesus said unto them, A prophet is not without honour, but in his own country, and among his own kin, and in his own house. And he could there do **no mighty work**, save that he laid his hands upon **a few sick folk**, and **healed them**. And he marveled because of their unbelief.*

Mark 6:3-6a

Familiarity, in essence, breeds contempt. Verse 5 says, "And He could there do no mighty work, save, [or except] that He laid His hands upon a few sick folk and healed them."

To put this in perspective, had we read this a few years ago, it would have sounded pretty fantastic to us that Jesus could heal *even a few* sick folk! Praise God for even the few. Because of our stunted experience with the power of God, it sounds pretty spectacular to us for Him to heal even a *few sick* folk, but by Scriptural definition, healing a few **was not** considered a mighty work of God. Mark adds in the verse following the above passage that Jesus marveled because of the unbelief of the onlookers (or "disbelief," "faithlessness").

The people thought, "This is just Jesus, the carpenter, the son of the carpenter, Mary's boy. We know Him. We know His brothers and His sisters. They still live here in town. He's a nobody. Where would He obtain the kind of power that they say He has? This can't be for real."

People will often say something negative like that to the person ministering, or to you about the person who prays for you. They don't realize it, but they want, consciously or unconsciously, to discourage and erode your faith. After all, the same thing happened to Jesus, in His own home town!

There was a *negative faith factor* involved for those people. The Jesus that they knew in Nazareth wasn't big enough to heal them. They lacked the understanding of how truly great He was. They did not appreciate the power that was residing in Him. They were adversely affected by their ignorance, by their stubborn spirits, and by their negative faith.

### Do You *Really* Want to be Healed?

Jesus asked a seemingly ridiculous question on two occasions of three blind men "What wilt thou that I shall do unto thee?" [i.e., "Do you *will* to be well?"] Blind

Bartimaeus and the others responded, "Lord, that I might receive my sight (that our eyes be opened)." Jesus then, of course, healed them. However, first He posed that question. Why?

Very often people who have spent a long time with an affliction learn both to live with it, and to accept it. It can become a subtle friend to them, or even a crutch, as it has prevented them having to function as other people do.

Jesus asked a similar question of the crippled man at the Pool of Bethesda, for the same reason.

*When Jesus saw him lie, and knew that he had been now a long time in that case, he saith unto him, **Wilt thou** be made whole?*
John 5:6

## Have You Availed Yourself of All The Help That Is Available?

How many individuals, sick today, might have been healed if they had not been left blind to the possibility of healing being real. Some, as discussed, have been prevented from seeking by prejudice, religious tradition, fear of loss of respect, or simply because they did not seek it. Or, as the above title suggests, they may have refused to go to places where healing was available and readily occurring. And, even more painful to imagine, how many were never offered prayer or teaching regarding healing?

This latter truth was brought forcefully home to me several years ago, when we saw the Lord open 120 deaf ears over about a three month period. One of these cases in particular left a great impression on me. An elderly man was brought to the meeting in August of 1986, when it so happened that the air conditioning in the room was malfunctioning. He sat in the back row, wearing what appeared to be a tan raincoat, or topcoat. He did not remove it, and he

58

appeared to scowl at me during the entire teaching.

When we began praying, someone brought him up for prayer. It turned out that he was stone deaf. He explained, in a thick German accent, that his injury was sustained in a foxhole in WWI, in France. He was deafened by an exploding mortar shell that also collapsed a tree on top him. He was pinned underneath the tree in his foxhole for three days until he was finally rescued. (Since he spoke with a German accent I assumed it was one of our shells that had deafened him.) Then the Lord worked a miracle; the Lord completely restored his hearing that night. This was more than just a miracle, it was many miracles wrapped into one. For instance, this healing required the recreation of the inner ear, and its delicate hearing mechanism, right there and then, as we prayed!

On the way home that night, I exclaimed to my wife, "Dear God, that poor man was *deaf for seventy years,* apparently because no one had bothered (or offered) to pray for him!"

### Returning to the Place Where Healing
### Was Initially Received

Along the same lines, I must confess to you that I am continually amazed, and still cannot understand, why individuals who have received tremendous miracles of healing at our meetings do not come back for prayer when they contract a new affliction. Or just to celebrate their healing from time to time. Certainly, many people do return, but there are some who do not, which has always been a mystery to me. I have discussed this with several other pastors who have experienced the same phenomenon.

On the other hand, we frequently do not encounter those who have been healed, until they have another physical need. One evening I had discussed this unusual facet of the healing ministry with a young woman attending our meeting for the first time. She commented, "I have difficulty believing that people don't come back until they have a need." The Lord then confirmed it for her, by having the first person who shared that evening say, "Bill, I don't know if you will remember me, I was here ten years ago and received a healing of my terrible stomach condition. I am back tonight, because I have injured my back."

Clearly there is an aspect of the human will, perhaps pride, that keeps people away from ministries that proclaim the power of God.

## Don't Believe a Diagnosis of "Hopeless," or "Incurable."

Don't believe all you hear. This is a crucial point, one which I have learned over the years through my own afflictions. When your disease is not able to be identified, (whether undiagnosed, incurable, or without a name), remember that the name of your Healer *is* known! And that His name is Jesus. Also remember that He knows precisely the name and nature of your condition. And finally, be aware that the doctors have been wrong many times. What is spoken through man is not what is spoken through the Spirit. My wife has been told on at least three different occasions that I would not live through the night, and I am still here!

One of the most powerful promises we have from God is that He will turn the greatest evil in our lives around, and transform them into the greatest good (Rom 8:28). And this happens in our darkest hours.

## Why Does it Take So Long?

Another difficult factor in healing is the need to persevere. Perseverance is a part of our responsibility, including "knocking, asking, and seeking," and then continuing to do so. It is an *aspect of faith*! We are encouraged to continue in fervent prayer, while at the same time to keep moving on, in spite of the opposition. Just like the woman with the flow of blood, who refused to give up in spite of opposition, until she was healed. (Matt. 9:20)

## Fight the Tendency to Give Up

You must keep on, keeping on. Do not give up! Remember those in the Scripture, who persevered. There was the case of the frustrated father who did not give up, even after the disciples were unable to deliver his son. Instead, he waited for Jesus and received the desired deliverance for his son (Mk. 9). You must determine to **never give up**! It would have been easy for me to have given up during the seven months that I was a "terminal cancer patient," or during my years in a wheelchair, but remember with me, that *God is faithful!*

## You Are Important

You *are important* to God. Jesus considered you important enough to die for you. If He thought you were important enough to die for, then why would He not also consider you important enough to heal?

Additional common blocks to healing that we run across are, "*I'm not good enough, I'm not worthy enough, I'm a nobody. What could I ever do for God?*"

I remember a woman who came to be baptized in the Holy Spirit. Before I could even pray with her, she started weeping, and said, "Why would God want to baptize me in the Holy Spirit? I'm only a housewife, what could I ever do for God?"

Praise God that He doesn't give us things on the basis of what we can do *for Him*, He gives us things on the basis of our need, and what He can *do for us*. It is on the basis of our need, not His need.  It is in the greatness of His love, mercy, and compassion that we can boldly receive all that He has for us.  This is why we are told that His love surpasses even our greatest knowledge of love! (Eph. 3:19).

## Healing Promises Are for You

I often respond to the argument, "God's healing promises aren't for me" with the following logic:

"Okay, I'll believe you, but first show me the verse in the Scripture that says that all the promises of healing are valid for everyone, except you?"  Thank goodness that the Bible uses the clear language that it does. There are no exceptions to Jesus' ministry.  And there is no business to be left unfinished in His earthly healing ministry!  Jesus is the same yesterday, today, and forever. (Heb. 13:8)

## "You Don't Deserve to be Healed."

No one is good enough to deserve anything from God. That is why there is an inherent problem with a religion of works. We receive on the basis of His grace, which is predicated upon His goodness and generosity, not ours! And His love and compassion is greater than our sins, and our failures.

## Choose To Be Teachable

Some people have unteachable spirits; their minds are set on their opinion. They are unwilling to learn truths about healing. They are closed; and they are, as a result, without faith. Make the decision to be open to the greater things of God.

If you have seen blocks in this chapter that you feel relate to you, you might start your prayer:

*Lord Jesus, I thank You for Your truth, and for the revelation of my own role in regard to my healing. I ask that you enable me to fully believe Your promises, cause me to walk in the light of Your truth, and to properly exercise my own will.*

* * *

"All of this sounds pretty good, but what if my time is up?"

# Chapter 5

# "Could It Be God's Will for Me to Die"

*The fear of the LORD is a fountain of life, to depart from the snares of death.* Prov. 14:27

Everyone who has faced a terminal illness has had to address this question, head on. Questions seem to continually arise, like "Am I to glorify God with my death?"and "Everyone has to die at some point, right?"

It is true that death is the one, still undefeated foe of man. However, the good news is that premature, unnatural death **was** dealt with by Jesus Christ both in His ministry and on the cross. How do we know God's will towards premature or unnatural death? Because Jesus raised to life three people who had died prematurely through sickness. This alone demonstrates both His will and the Father's will on the matter.

These, and similar issues, are addressed below in the context of death for the Christian.

## "I'm To Glorify God with My Death"

I experienced this block early on in my battle with cancer, thinking it was God's will for me to die. Somehow, I reasoned, this would bring Him glory. But then I realized, as David did in Psalms, "What glory is there for you in my death, Lord?"

*What profit is there in my blood, when I go down to the pit? Shall the dust praise thee? Shall it declare thy truth?* Psa. 30:9

65

God gets far more glory from my living. Compare the two, death and life, and ask "Which one is logically more glorifying to God, the Creator of life?" The Lord will clearly benefit in a greater sense from the testimony of my healing and my preserved life, because it brings the greatest recognition of His power, and glory due His name. He also gets the glory when I am able to continue to offer Him my love, my worship and my adoration. And He will benefit from all my years of future service given to Him from a position of free-will. David recognized this truth.

## "But Everyone Has To Die At Some Point"

A young woman who came to my prayer room for healing posed an interesting question. "Mr. Banks, How can you pray for *anyone* to be healed? I was taught, and have always believed, that when someone died it was the will of God."

I responded with the answer, which the Lord quickened to me, "That's a good question, but haven't you read in the Scripture where Jesus said that Satan is a liar, a thief and *a murderer*? How could Satan be *a murderer*, if everyone who died, died in accordance with the will of God? Furthermore, if I were to pull out a gun right now, and kill you, that *could not be* God's will! He would not have me break one of His commandments ("Thou shalt not kill") in order to accomplish His will for your life."

Logically, if God the Father is the Creator of life and identifies Himself as our Healer, if Jesus healed all who sought healing from Him, and if the Holy Spirit continues to minister healing today, it is clear that sickness, disease and premature death are neither within His will, nor of His doing. In fact, they are implied to be acts of murder by Satan.

She then countered with the argument, "But everybody is going to die sometime."

*...it is appointed unto men once to die...*
Heb. 9:27

Yes, of course, this is true. Everyone will one day die. However, our death should be according to God's will, and His timing, with our life complete and not cut short.

*Thou shalt come to thy grave in a **full age**, like as a shock of corn cometh in his season.* Job 5:26

When is one's time up? Some die when they have completed their allotted time. Scripture suggests a normal lifespan of seventy or perhaps eighty years (Psa. 90:10), and God promises a long life to His own. On each of the three occasions when I was told that I would not live through the night, I took great comfort from the following verse from the great protection Psalm.

*With **long life** will I satisfy him, and show him my salvation.* Psa. 91:16

However, death is still inevitable.

## Death Is, As Yet, An Undefeated Foe

Death is the only foe that has not been destroyed in the strictest sense. Disease, *premature death*, eternal separation from God, all these were defeated when Jesus cried from the cross: "It is finished." Death in the normal, "old age" sense, however, will not be defeated until the Messiah returns, and the mortal becomes immortal.

Extensions of lifespan, however, may be granted to individuals. As an example, Hezekiah was afflicted with sickness, but was granted an additional fifteen years of life by God. This is a Scriptural fact (Isa. 38). Yet after his fifteen-year extension, Hezekiah did die. There is a time to live and a time to die.

Likewise, there is victory over premature death through Jesus. Take, for instance, the premature death of Lazarus. He died young. The Lord recognized this, and brought him back to life. Even Lazarus, however, whom Jesus miraculously healed and raised from the dead, eventually died; death, for the present, is a natural part of life.

It is not the will of God for any of His children to perish. Our God, who repeatedly tells us that He heeds the cry of innocent blood, certainly does not desire death for any innocent or righteous person, and even takes no pleasure in the death of the unrighteous! Consider His words:

*As I live, saith the Lord GOD, I have **no pleasure in the death of the wicked; but that the wicked turn from his way and live**: turn ye, turn ye from your evil ways; for why will ye die...?* Ezek. 33:11

*For I have **no pleasure in the death of him that dieth**, saith the Lord GOD: wherefore turn yourselves, and live ye.* Ezek. 18:32

*Have I any pleasure at all **that the wicked should die**? saith the Lord GOD: and not that he should return from his ways, and live?* Ezek. 18:23

His view of death remains the same in the New Testament as well.

*Even so it is **not the will** of your Father which is in heaven, that one of these little ones **should perish**.* Mat. 18:14

*The Lord is not slack concerning his promise, as some men count slackness; but is longsuffering to us-ward, not willing that any should perish*, *but that all should come to repentance.*                    2 Pet. 3:9

## Premature or Unnatural Death

From Scripture we learn that it is possible to die prematurely through sickness. Why do some die early? For one thing, not everyone wants to be well, as we have considered. Second, some choose to go home to the Lord, to end their pain, their suffering. They are praying for a quick death, and that is their prerogative, a choice of their free will.

Scripture clearly teaches that premature death is possible – that it's possible to die *before our time*. There are several reasons given for premature death, other than death by sickness. Allow me to share a few of them with you.

*Be not righteous over much; neither make thyself over wise:* **why** *shouldest thou* **destroy thyself***?*
                                      Eccl. 7:15-16

The writer is saying that *we* can destroy ourselves by being overly wise (or thinking that we are). He continues,

*Be not over much wicked, neither be thou foolish: why shouldest thou die* **before thy time***?*        Eccl. 7:17

Notice that he connects being foolish with dying early. *"Why shouldst thou die before thy time?"* Obviously, God is telling us several things here. First that there is a proper, appointed time period for man to live. In Psalm 91:16, David writes, "With long life will I satisfy him and show him My salvation." Second, there are some who through lifestyle choices bring an early death on themselves.

God's plan is simply this: a good long life for His people. But some can die before their time, and some of these bring an early death upon themselves. The most obvious way is found in Proverbs, where we read,

*The lips of the righteous feed many: but fools die for want of wisdom.* Prov. 10:21

What is wisdom? *Jesus* is wisdom, the Word of God is wisdom, God's truth is wisdom. If we are outside of His salvation or pursuing another form of salvation, we are inviting death. Fools die for want of wisdom, that is, for a lack of Jesus Christ. Fortunately, there are examples of foolish individuals who choose not to remain foolish, and they are rewarded. They recognized their need and cried out to God who responded with healing and deliverance.

*Fools because of their transgression, and because of their iniquities, are afflicted. Their soul abhorreth all manner of meat; and they draw near unto the gates of death. Then they cry unto the LORD in their trouble, and he saveth them out of their distresses. He sent his word, and healed them, and* **delivered them from their destructions**. Psa. 107:17-20

Fools are seen here to be dying because of their iniquities, but when they cry out to God, He hears and saves them from *death* and *destruction*. This implies that they were granted an extension of years to their lives. Notice another important key: "He sent His Word," which was His agent for accomplishing their healing and deliverance. His *Word* (Jesus, the *Logos*) preserved their lives!

Elsewhere in Psalms it says, "*This poor man cried and the Lord heard his cry and saved him.*" When we are desperate enough to cry out to the Lord, He hears us and answers us. Holy desperation often drives us into healing contact with the Lord.

Another basis for dying prematurely is *acceptance,* which would fall in part under the general heading of free-will. I was one, who in 1970, accepted the death sentence pronounced over me by the doctors. I blindly chose to believe man, rather than the Word of God, of which I was ignorant by my own foolishness. I did not know what I should have known, that the broken body of Jesus has atoned for my sickness, and that Jesus healed all who came to Him.

Still another cause for dying prematurely is, as the Scripture warns: *You have not because you ask not!*

## Everyone *Will* Meet Jesus Someday

Some of us will, indeed, meet Jesus through the doorway of death, and some of us living today will, I suspect, meet him when He comes to catch us to Himself. It appears that we are getting close to the end of the age. So there *are some* who will not taste of death.

> *For the Lord himself shall descend from heaven with a shout, with the voice of the archangel, and with the trump of God: and the dead in Christ shall rise first: Then we which **are alive** and remain shall be caught up together with them in the clouds, to meet the Lord in the air: and so shall we ever be with the Lord.*
>
> 1 Thes. 4:16-17

There's one more facet of this issue we need to discuss. We know that most Christians today, even true Christians (not to mention the mere professing Christians) are living *substandard* Christian lives. I say that of myself as well as of the rest. That is, we are not living in the fullness of God's potential for us, and in the fullness of the power of the Holy Spirit. We should not expect to die like the unsaved, and we should not live in fear of death. Furthermore, we should expect to see the power of the Holy Spirit demonstrated over the evil spirits of premature death and sickness.

I submit to you, that no matter how far you think you have attained up the ladder of progress with God, wherever you are, you're going to find one of these days that there is somebody on the rung ahead of you saying, "Come on up here, it's better than you know."

## Death is Deferred

Long life is God's promise and provision. Seventy or eighty years is established as the normal minimum lifespan.

The Old Testament gives several exciting examples of long life. Recognize that these men lived after the flood, when lifespans were greatly shortened.

> *And Moses was* **an hundred and twenty years old** *when he died: his eye was not dim, nor his natural force abated.* Deut. 34:7

**Moses** was one hundred-twenty the day he died, and his vital forces weren't abated; his vision wasn't even dimmed. He was a vitally active human being up to the day that he "dropped." **Caleb** was eighty-five and still going strong, until he died.

Obviously, there does come a time, eventually, for all of us to go home to be with the Lord. Eventually these bodies of ours are going to wear out, and a time may come when we would prefer to be at home with the Lord. When that time arrives, I would suggest that there is a *way to die*, and a *way not to die*. There's a Christian way to die, and a substandard Christian way to die.

# Christian Deaths

Death for the Christian is not something to be feared, but rather in due time to be embraced. When the time comes, death will not be unlike taking passage on an ocean liner to a desired heavenly port. Heaven is a far more desirable and wonderful place than any resort location on this beautiful planet.

*For to me to live is Christ, and to **die is gain**.*
Phil. 1:21

*Precious in the sight of the LORD is the death of his saints.*
Psa. 116:15

On the other hand, "old-age" death is an enemy that has been defeated in some fashion for Christians, because we do not die like the unsaved. Death need not be feared, it need not be terrible, and it certainly is not the end of existence for a Christian. After all, we will reign with Christ some day, implying the best is yet to come! Because Christians have hope, death for us is more like a graduation day; it is a precious time to the Lord, our heavenly parent.

*O death, where is thy sting? O grave, where is thy victory?*
1 Cor. 15:55

It is logical, and should be obvious to us, that there would be a distinction made between the death of an individual who knows God, and one who does not. In Scripture, there are actually two different words used in describing death. The word most commonly used in Greek for death is *"thanatos,"* (*than'-at-os*). This is the word applied to those who do not know Jesus. This is also the death, which Jesus tasted for all mankind. Furthermore, Jesus promised that some "shall not taste of death (*thanatos*) till they see the kingdom of God."

However, when describing believers, they are said to *"fall asleep"* (*"koimao,"* *koy-mah'-o:* "put to sleep"), like Stephen in Acts 7:60. Similarly the daughter of Jairus (Lk. 8:41) was "awakened from *sleep*," as was Lazarus (John 11:11), even though in both cases the onlookers were absolutely convinced beyond any doubt that the individual was dead. Further, in describing the abuses of Communion at Corinth, Paul mentions that "many *sleep*" because they partook of the Lord's Supper "unworthily." It is obvious that the Holy Spirit wants the children of God to know that there is nothing to fear from Christian death.

Similarly, death need not be feared, because we have the helmet of salvation. I recall, when I was in the hospital over thirty years ago, and they told me I was going to die of cancer, I really didn't fear death. I had on "the helmet of salvation," and knew that even if Satan took his worst shot at me, and were to literally destroy my flesh, he still could not win. The ultimate victory was the Lord's, and this victory was also mine. I was going home to be with Jesus, regardless of what Satan did to me.

Two stories will illustrate the principle of the Christian way of dying: one is second-hand, involving a ministry experience of Kenneth Hagin, and the other stories have been related directly to me through personal accounts.

Kenneth Hagin and some of his elders went out to call on a woman of his congregation who was in her eighties, who had cancer. She had been opened up at the hospital, and sent home to die, given a week to live. When they went to her house, knocked on the door, the husband ushered them into the woman's room. Brother Hagin announced, "Sister so-and-so, we're here to pray for your healing."

She said, "Oh Brother Hagin, I'm eighty-some years old. You've got a lot of people in the church that need to be healed; I'm old and it's my time to go."

He said, (these are his words, not my words) "Well if you're going to die, at least die like a Christian."

She said, "What do you mean?"

He said, "Die *well*, don't die sick. Let us pray that cancer out of your body, and then, if you want to die, go ahead and die. You can just go home to be with the Lord, but don't go as a result of cancer."

She said, "Well okay..."

So they prayed for her. Later the report came that she was serving in South America as a missionary!

## Wigglesworth Raises A Dead Woman

I personally heard this next case from a dear sweet saint, who also told me she had received the baptism in the Spirit under the ministry of Smith Wigglesworth. She began her story by saying, "Mentioning Smith Wigglesworth will date me..."

And then she proceeded to say that Wigglesworth was summoned to the house of a woman of his parish who had been quite sick. When he arrived there about eight o'clock in the evening and knocked at the door, the husband said, "Oh Brother Wigglesworth, you got here too late. She died over an hour ago."

Smith prayed silently on the front porch, "Lord, you didn't send me out here to pray for a dead woman." So he told the grieving husband, "I want to see the body."

"Smith then went up to her bedroom," and she added, "By this time the body was already stiff, so he picked her up and stood her against the wardrobe."

She continued, "Smith stood the woman against the wardrobe and said, "In the Name of Jesus Christ of Nazareth, I command you to walk! In the Name of Jesus Christ of Nazareth, I command you to walk! In the Name of Jesus

Christ of Nazareth, WALK!"

"The first thing that woman heard," she told me, "was him saying, 'In the Name of Jesus Christ, WALK!' and she walked across the room."

That dead lady was healed; was restored, brought back to life. Obviously, she had died prematurely. I might also point out that each of the people whom Jesus raised from the dead, that we read of in Scripture, had *died prematurely*.

Finally, let me share with you a beautiful story that occurred in Oklahoma. The woman who told me this story was a first hand participant in it, and it again illustrates the principle of Christian death.

## Suspended Animation

The woman began her story, "I live in a home, and behind it I have a cottage that I rent out. At that time I had it rented to a little old lady who was in her nineties. I would take the little old lady to town every week or so to shop. On one occasion as we were driving to town, the woman asked me, "You're a Christian aren't you?"

While still driving I said, "Yes."

The little lady then asked, "You believe that God answers prayer, don't you?"

I replied, "Yes, I surely do."

Next, the little lady asked, "Do you think He could answer a prayer for me?"

Confidently the woman replied, "Well, I'm sure He could. What would you like to pray about?"

She explained, "Well I'm getting close to the time when I'm going to die, and every person in my family has died a horrible painful lingering death.." Haltingly she asked, "Do you think that we could pray, and ask God that when my time comes, that I could have a quick and painless passing, so that I wouldn't have to suffer any pain?"

"I don't see why not." The woman replied, as she pulled the car over to the side of the road. They prayed that prayer, and then continued into town.

The woman relating the story to me said, "I didn't think anything more about it. However, one day several months later, I realized that I hadn't seen the little old lady the day before. So, I went out and knocked on her front door. When I didn't get any answer, I went around to the back and knocked on the kitchen door. When I still didn't get an answer, I looked in the kitchen window. I saw her standing at the kitchen sink. I knocked repeatedly on the window, and still couldn't get her attention, so I called the police. The police came, and then called in the coroner. The coroner was dumbfounded. He told me, 'I have never seen anything like this. That woman is dead, standing at the kitchen sink with a tea cup in one hand, and a dish towel in the other. She couldn't have felt *one twinge of pain*, or she'd have dropped the dish towel, or she'd have dropped the tea cup, or she'd have fallen over. Obviously, she didn't feel a thing!'"

That's what I mean, when I say, we all too often settle for substandard Christian lives. We don't dare to take God at His Word, and ask boldly for the things we desire, or even the things we need. God is a miracle-working God. The storehouse of heaven will never be emptied, it's never going to be depleted or strained by our making requests.

Incidentally, every time that I have taught on this subject around the country someone has come up to me afterwards, and related a personal account of a Christian relative's passing, such as "My Uncle Ed was reading his Bible the night that he passed away, and we found him the next morning with a page half way turned, as if he had been frozen in that position. Everyone was amazed that he could have so peaceful a passing."

## "I Wish I Were Dead."

How often have we heard this said by others, or perhaps, even by ourselves. What we have unthinkingly done is made a covenant with death. We have spoken a 'word curse' against ourselves. This is a very serious matter. So serious, that God Himself made provision for fathers to disannul improper vows made by daughters, and husbands to set aside those vowed by wives (Numb. 30). It is necessary to reverse those self-inflicted curses of death. When we come to our senses, and repent, there is good news, as prophetically stated in the words of Isaiah:

> ...*your covenant with death shall be disannulled, and your agreement with hell shall not stand...* Isa.8:18

## "What about Those Who Do Die?"

If they are Christians, they will go home to be with the Lord and will enjoy pleasures that we can only imagine. Our task is to be sure that no one perishes without Jesus.

I find I often learn more from my mistakes and failures, than I do from my successes. Let me share some truths I gained from a healing that didn't seem to work.

Years ago, I went to a hospital in Missouri to pray for a lady in her early fifties. She had been diagnosed with terminal cancer and had attended one of our meetings and received Jesus as her Savior. A week or so later, I learned that she had experienced a major setback, and was hospitalized. On a Monday I went to visit her, anointed her with oil and had her sit up in her bed, so that I could hold her feet. The Lord lengthened her short leg and her pain left. When I returned on Wednesday, she looked quite discouraged and told me, "My veins have collapsed and they have said I will have to have an operation in order for them to be able to insert an IV."

That didn't seem too difficult to me, so I said, "Lets just pray about that."

Before we were able to pray, a Resident Doctor rushed into the room followed by a nurse carrying gauze and supplies loaded almost to her chin. Brusquely, the Resident attempted to dismiss me saying, "Would you mind waiting outside, we have to perform a 'cut-down.'"

Responding with a boldness that surprised myself, I replied, "Would *you* mind waiting outside, until we finish praying?"

As soon as they left, she asked, "Do you want me to sit up so you can hold my feet again?

I laughed and told her, "No, I think the Lord can give us an even better sign." So I prayed, "Lord, please expand my sister's veins, so that they can find a vein without having to perform the surgery."

I then walked out of the room. Passing the Resident and nurse sitting on a gurney in the hall, I told them, "Okay now you can go in there, and find that vein *with a needle!*"

I couldn't believe how joyful I felt, as I hurried down the hall to find a phone to call my wife to get some prayer in agreement for the miracle; the miracle for which I had just stuck out my neck. All the pay phones on her floor were in use. So I hurried down to the lobby to try to find an open phone. As soon as I got off the elevator, I ran into a close friend of the woman whom I'd just left. Before I could get a word in, she starting telling me how hopeless the situation was, and how they had notified the family about her collapsed veins. Just as I began explaining the current situation to her, the woman's daughter then rushed into the hospital lobby and joined us. I was about to explain what we had just prayed upstairs, when I felt a tap on my shoulder. When I turned around, the Resident was standing there beaming from ear to ear. He said, "I want to shake your hand." And he did.

"Why did you want to shake my hand?" I asked totally perplexed.

"Because, we found that vein WITH A NEEDLE!" He announced loudly enough to be heard by everyone in the lobby. "Then you know that you just saw a miracle, don't you?" I asked.

"You know that *I know*, that I just saw a miracle!" He said, still pumping my hand.

Needless to say, I left that hospital floating.

I wasn't able to get back to the hospital again, until Saturday of that week. When I reached her room, the door was shut, so I asked at the desk if I could enter. The head nurse asked, "Are you family?"

I replied, "No, I'm her minister."

She said, "I'm sorry, she passed away at three o'clock this morning."

My knees went weak. I was stunned, on the verge of tears. How could this be? I was so shocked I mumbled a "Thank you," went to my car and drove west for half an hour, trying to make sense out of what had happened. Finally, I pulled off the road under a huge oak, and opened my Bible, looking for answers. My glance immediately fell on the following words in Psalms.

> *Precious in the sight of the LORD is the death of his saints.* Psa. 116:15

As I prayerfully continued seeking answers, I decided that God apparently knew that this woman, as a brand new baby Christian, needed that special blessing of a miracle to be able to hold on, and to persevere unto the end, in faith. In His mercy, God settled for a premature death in Him.

Why is it that some get angelic visitations and special miracles and others apparently do not? This case may give a clue, some need them to be enabled to persevere to the end.

Death, for now, is a natural part of life.

* * *

If you have seen blocks in this chapter that you feel relate to you, you might start your prayer:

*Lord Jesus, I thank You for sparing my life thus far and allowing me to discover the truths about You that I have. I thank you for the knowledge that You do not want me to die prematurely. Help me to live for You.*

* * *

"What you say sounds valid, but on the other hand, I've heard people say...."

# Chapter 6

# "Could *They* Be Right?"

**The Principle Is: "You Can't Believe Them!"**

Whenever someone attempts to disprove or refute healing, or any other aspect of the Word of God, beware. And when the argument includes, "*They say...*" always ask who "they" are. Determine why those people are arguing against healing, and why they hold their particular version on the truth.

*Thus have ye made the commandment of God of none effect by your tradition.*                    Mat. 15:6b

These individuals often use circuitous reasoning and rationalization to explain away a lack of power on *their* part. I have discovered over the past three decades, that every ministry or denomination will either have a ministry demonstrating power, and offer healing and deliverance, or they will have a theology *explaining why* they do not have power in their ministry, including healing and deliverance.

*Having a form of godliness, but **denying the power** thereof: **from such turn away**.*                    2 Tim. 3:5

In other words, if ministers, elders, seminarians, and others do not have the faith or the belief in God's absolute will to heal, or to work miracles, then they will not see the power of God to heal in their own lives or through their ministries. And then their theology regarding healing will rest on the denial of the power of God to do great things.

In contrast, Paul came...

*...not with enticing words of man's wisdom,* **but in demonstration of the Spirit and of power***: That your faith should not stand in the wisdom of men, but in the power of God.*                                     1 Cor. 2:4-5

As soon as you begin to seek healing, you will inevitably encounter "*them*" – people in every day life who are always providing opinions on healing. They are the ones who say, "Everyone doesn't get healed," therefore implying, "Don't *you* expect to get healed." Because in their experience healing hasn't always worked, then God to them is not consistent in His healing promises. And they say such to you, with the clear implication that healing *does not work* more often *than it does.* Or that healing is no longer for the Church today.

They are wrong, or they are lying, intentionally or unintentionally. Therefore, we need a true Rock to stand on, especially when these people and their storms come and attack our faith. And that Rock is the Word of God.

Jesus promises healing for you in His Word, as we have seen in the case of the leper in Luke chapter five, and in many other cases. Your basis for being healed is not because I was healed, or because someone else was healed, nor because I say that Jesus is the Healer. Your basis for faith to be healed is the fact that *the Word of God says* that He is the Healer.

There are several variations and several sources from which you will hear, "*they say.*" The first source is family, friends and loved ones. These tend to be the hardest to deal with, because you know that the people speaking to you love you, and you feel that they really have your best interests at heart. However, once they begin to speak, you can feel your faith being eroded.

Some of you are familiar with what I referred to in my first book, *Alive Again!*, as the "cousin Sally syndrome." In 1970, I ventured out for the first time after my cancer surgery to a Christmas party for my wife's knitting club, basically a group of women who were the wives of several of my college friends. I tottered into that Christmas gathering and immediately realized, from the expressions on their faces that they were shocked to see how bad I looked.

My college roommate, who was probably my closest friend, came up to me and said, "Gee, I hear you've had cancer. I'm sure sorry to hear it."

I mustered a response, "Yeah, well, I'm doing a little better, and I'm trusting the Lord to heal me."

"Oh, that's great," He said. "But, let me tell you about my cousin Sally." Then he started telling me the story about poor cousin Sally, and how she suffered, and lingered, and suffered even more...it went on, and on, and on. Fortunately, as soon as he started the story, I knew this wasn't my friend speaking to me. It was Satan speaking to me through him, trying to erode what little faith I had. So I kept smiling and pretending to be listening to his story, but all the while praying in the Spirit. I prayed in tongues inwardly, as loudly as I could, trying to drown him out within my prayers.

When he finally finished his account, with a look of shock upon his face, he asked, "Why did I tell you that story? You certainly didn't need to hear that!"

I knew why. It was not my friend that cared for me who was speaking to me, but rather Satan speaking through him. Just like he spoke to the Lord through the mouth of Peter (Matt. 16:23). The devil was attempting to erode what little faith I possessed at that time

You are going to find that when you attempt to stand in faith on the Word of God, Satan will do his best to make you fall from faith, and from trusting God for victory.

It sometimes becomes downright blatant and obvious. When we first began trusting God for my healing from cancer, my wife Sue would return from the grocery store, and relate bizarre stories about "how the women in line in front of her at the checkout counter would begin to discuss cancer cases." And how she could, at that moment, begin to feel her faith dwindle, as they dwelt upon the horrible symptoms and related all the gory details.

Satan tries to rub your nose in those things that tend to erode your faith. We have to make the decision not to accept whatever negatives *"they say"*: to make our stand and to reject them, even if they come from our friends, family, or loved ones.

If you have just found out that you've got diabetes, and no one else knows it, you may go to a family gathering and suddenly find that two of your aunts begin to talk about someone else who has diabetes and how terrible the symptoms are. That's often the way Satan chooses to work. He doesn't always come at you in a direct frontal attack. It's the subtle peripheral attack, when he blindsides you, picking away at your faith, in order to eradicate it; that's always the most effective for him.

Another source of *"they say"* is the medical profession. This is another hard one to deal with, because they are professionals, and you have paid them money for their opinions and diagnoses.

Years ago, when the doctor told me I was going to die, I didn't question him. He was an authority figure, a professional. I had paid him money to treat me. I assumed he was telling me the truth. At that time I was an insurance salesman. If he had asked me a question about insurance, I'd have told him the truth. So I expected to be getting the best advice that money could buy, and some of the best doctors in St. Louis told me I was going to die. I believed *them.* Why doubt *them*?

I simply accepted what *"they"* said, which is often a disastrous mistake. Even doctors will often recommend getting a second opinion. You especially do not want to believe them when *"they"* say something that is in conflict with the Word of God. In most cases, *"they"* aren't familiar with the spiritual realm.

As an example, my friend Rick had a problem with gallstones. He saw them on the X-rays, but after his wife had us pray about the condition, they just disappeared. The doctors had told him that, medically, there was no possible way for them to have dissolved, or to have disappeared on their own. *"They"* didn't believe it, until they opened him up through surgery and found that the gallstones were gone – there were no more stones. So they asked Rick, "What happened? How do you explain this?"

He replied, "I can't explain it, but my wife has been attending a prayer meeting where they have been praying for my healing."

The third category of *"they say"* that you will run into are well meaning, outwardly religious people, but you still cannot believe them, either. They also lie, intentionally or unintentionally, as we will see in a moment.

First, it is important to point out that sometimes, whether consciously or subconsciously, these well intentioned people do not want you to get ahead of them spiritually, or grow in an area of faith. It's threatening for them. If you are growing in God faster than they are, or if they feel they're not growing at all, then *they* feel as if they are failing. And, of course, no one wants to fail.

An illustration of an intentional lie would be if someone tells you, as a sick person, something about another person who is sick. Some fact that is deeply personal, like "they are desperately seeking the Lord for their healing." Recognize that you and I cannot see hearts, or read the minds of others; only God can see hearts and only God knows whether that patient is really praying to be healed. Sometimes patients have had just too much – too much treatment, too much pain, too much suffering – and so they're actually praying for an end of suffering, and to die. Were this to be the case, then the lie planted in your mind would become a block to your faith, if the other person who is sick remains ill, or dies.

## Case of A Terminally Ill Teenager

Several years ago a young boy of about fourteen, who was diagnosed with terminal cancer, was brought to one of our meetings for prayer. Sadly, this was just a few weeks before he died. The boy allowed us pray for him, but I sensed that he was only going through the motions.

A few weeks after his death, his best friend told his own parents, who in turn told the boy's mother, that the cancer patient had said in confidence that he was praying to die. He explained to his friend that he was praying for an end to the pain and suffering, and that he wanted to go home to be with the Lord. He was praying that he wouldn't have to undergo any more treatments, or hospitalization.

But those on the outside looking in saw a family claiming a healing, and a mother who in her church was actively professing and claiming her son's victory. Judging from the outward appearances, the world (*they*) would say, "Well you see it didn't work." But those people who were saying, "It didn't work," couldn't see the heart of the candidate.

## Sunshine or Rain

If today you pray for sunshine, and I pray for rain, it really matters little which of our prayers gets answered. We will assume that God can't answer both our prayers; it's either going to be a sunny day, or it's going to rain, and the outcome isn't vital.

On the other hand, let's assume that you are praying for me to be healed, and I am praying to die. I think my prayer as the victim (or prospective "*healee*") tends to take precedent over the prayer of someone else, who is praying for me. The prayer of the sick person and *the will* of that individual are crucially important to the outcome. That's a major reason why it's so important that we be sure that we are in one accord with the individual for whom we're praying.

Again, this illustrates why we simply cannot believe what "*they say*," because *they* don't know what all is involved regarding the thinking and will of the sick person.


## Case of A Woman in Wheelchair

Another example that illustrates this same principle is the case of a woman who came to one of our meetings about fifteen years ago, in a wheelchair. Several people suggested that she be prayed for, but when I started to anoint her with oil, she interrupted me. She asked, "Could I talk to you first?"

When I took her aside into another room privately, I asked, "What would you like to talk about?"

"Well, I've been in this wheelchair for many years, and," she continued, a bit embarrassed. "I've got to be honest with you, I'm afraid to be healed. I'm afraid if I were to be healed, that I might lose being the center of attention. I'd have to start doing housework again, and I'm afraid I might lose my husband." She sighed, and stammered, "I...I may be wrong, but I'm halfway convinced that he's staying with me, just because I'm an invalid, and I'm afraid I might lose him if I were to be healed. I'm afraid my children wouldn't have the same love for me that they have for me now."

She was being brutally honest, and that's the best way to approach God – to be brutally honest. We have to face all the doubts and the negatives. Regrettably, she decided against prayer.

## Are You Willing to Be Completely Honest Before God?
### All The Facts Are Not Observable

Jesus asked seemingly strange questions of the crippled man at the Pool of Bethesda, "Wilt thou be [do you want to be] made whole?" He posed a similar question to the two blind men (Mat. 20:30), and to blind Bartimaeus (Mark 10:46, Luke 18:35): "What will ye that I shall do unto you?"

Seemingly foolish questions! Why would He ask whether they wanted to be made well, or what they wanted Him to do for them? It is obvious, Jesus knew what we are learning – just because someone has an affliction, doesn't necessarily mean that they want to be well. Some people don't want to be well.

Later, I discovered another facet of this problem in the case of a woman who had previously received a wonderful miracle healing.

## A Woman Who Did Not Want to Be Healed

A woman who was losing her sight came to our Thursday night prayer meeting. She had "tunnel vision," and could just see a small spot directly in front of her. She had been to a prestigious university hospital, where they had tested her and diagnosed her condition as macular degeneration. They said her case was hopeless, incurable. There was absolutely nothing they could do for her; that she would

90

simply have to wait until she went blind. The only suggestion they could offer was for her to learn Braille quickly, so that she would be better able to cope with her blindness. Not a very faith-building recommendation.

She came to the meeting, received prayer and her sight was completely restored! She told us a month later that she went back to the hospital, and they had written her up as the first-ever documented healing of macular degeneration. Praise God!

About five years later, she happened to be in our bookstore and asked quietly across the counter, "Pray for me, that I have a quick recovery."

Surprised, I asked, "Quick recovery from what?"

She said, "Well I'm going to have surgery next Tuesday on my hip."

A couple of my employees standing nearby heard her request, recognized her, and knew of the fabulous miracle that God had worked for her in the past. They suggested, "Why don't you just have Bill pray for you."

She agreed quietly, "Oh yeah, yeah. Why don't we do that."

We went into the prayer room, where I offered her a chair. I was preparing to anoint her with oil, but as I started to do so, she seemed to duck away. I knew in my spirit there was something wrong. I wiped the oil from my finger, because I sensed she wasn't a candidate for healing. I didn't know why, but I knew that she wasn't.

So I asked her, "You don't really want to be healed, do you?"

She began to weep. "No." She explained, "I'm a school teacher. I've been a school teacher for over thirty years. Now, I'm almost fifty-nine and I hate my job. I used to love it, but now I hate it. I have to pass these kids that can't read, can't write, can't do math. They won't let us flunk them, even though half the kids I'm passing can't read or write."

She continued, "I absolutely hate what I'm doing. There's no longer any respect in the classrooms...It's torture for me to go to work." She concluded firmly, "If I have this hip operation, they told me that I'll get six months recovery leave after the surgery. That means, by then I'll be fifty-nine and a half and I can take early retirement, and I'll never have to go back to that classroom again."

Well, it's perfectly alright with me that she didn't want to go back to her job. But the thing that makes me livid is for somebody to lie before God, and say, "I'm praying to be healed," or "I want prayer to be healed," when that is not the case at all. They don't want to be healed any more than they want a leg cut off.

She was lying by her will and her actions, potentially bringing reproach upon her God and His ability to heal. And that is what infuriates me. There are a surprising number of similar cases that I hear about, where people have professed wanting to be healed, who have been going through the "prayer" routine, who were, in fact, really praying or hoping for the exact opposite. That, I believe, is what the Scripture speaks of when the Word of God says,

*For the name of God is blasphemed among the Gentiles through you, as it is written.*      Rom. 2:24

That is what brings reproach upon the kingdom of God, and gives the enemies of healing, the enemies of Christ, the opportunity to say, "You see, it doesn't really work. Those people promoting healing don't know what they're talking about."

This case also illustrates the extreme importance of being able to be in one accord with the person in need. You cannot possibly be in one accord, if one party is not in agreement to be healed. Praying in agreement is tremendously powerful, but it works only when the Holy Spirit leads two people into a harmonious agreement for prayer.

My favorite story of *"they say"* beautifully and mercifully illustrates this third category of people that we encounter, those who say one thing but do another.

## Dying Woman in North St. Louis

Thirty years ago, I was invited to visit a woman in North St. Louis who was dying of terminal cancer. The invitation to pray for her came through my accountant, who told me he had known the woman for years. He described her as, "A dear lady. She believes in healing, her father, and grandfather both believed in healing and in fact, had started churches, or held healing services, in the northern part of the city."

He continued, repeating himself, "She believes in healing; and everybody in North St. Louis is praying for her, but she isn't getting any better. They've sent her home from the hospital to die, and given her less than a week to live. Will you come and pray for her?"

I agreed, and we went together, to see the woman. We walked into her bedroom, where she was resting in a hospital-type bed. In less than five minutes after I walked into that bedroom, the Lord showed me what the problem was. I went over to her bedside, and asked her gently, "Have you asked God to heal you?"

She began to cry, and said, "No, I haven't."

I slowly recovered from the obvious shock. Had she died, everyone in North St. Louis who had been praying for her would have said, "You see, God doesn't heal everybody, because He didn't heal that dear, sweet, saint, Mrs. _____." And those who were earnestly seeking her healing would have had their own faith damaged in some way.

I asked, "Why? Why haven't you asked? Don't you know that everybody in North St. Louis is praying for you to be healed?"

She replied, "Oh, I know it, and I feel terrible about it."

She added, "Honey, I'm nearly seventy-two and God has blessed me so greatly." She explained, "When I was a young girl of about fourteen, I was a cripple. I had a twisted spine. I was all doubled over. I read the first article that came out on Kathryn Kuhlman." (She said it appeared either in *Better Homes* or *Good Housekeeping*.) "As I read that article, the power of God went down my spine three times like a bolt of electricity, and I felt my back snap back into place. Later, I went over to the hospital, and they checked me out again, and then they wrote me up as a medically diagnosed, miraculous cure!"

"God did all that for me," she continued now smiling. "My husband is saved; my children are saved; my grandchildren and great grandchildren are all saved; and they're all walking with God.....You see how tremendously I've been blessed. *I* just *can't* ask God for anything more."

We then dealt with the obvious fallacy in her theology, as to which was going to give God more glory: her tapping into His strength and healing power, or allowing herself to die and let God appear to fail in front of all those people in North St. Louis.

I shared some Scriptures with her. Then, when she agreed, and we came into one accord that it would give God far more glory for her to be healed than for her to die, we prayed for her healing. As I left her bedroom that afternoon, there was no visible sign of any change in her, other than the fact that she was smiling as I left, and had not been, when I arrived.

Two years later I was conducting a healing service in a church, and her husband came up afterwards and introduced himself. He reminded me of the case, and apologized that they hadn't kept in touch. He reported, "Within a week she was out of bed; within thirty days of your visit they could not find a trace of cancer in her body! And," he added, "We had the two best years we ever had in our married life together. Then one night she passed away in her sleep, so quietly that she didn't even awaken me."

He found her "asleep" beside him the following morning. He explained that an autopsy was performed and they could find *no trace of cancer in her body*.

Again, had one taken the story on the surface and believed what "they say," we would have been in Satan's snare, because *they* often do not tell the truth.

Before closing this section, I want to give you a scriptural confirmation why you cannot believe *them* – the unbelieving majority.

*While he yet spake, there cometh one from the ruler of the synagogue's house, saying to him, Thy daughter is dead; trouble not the Master. But when Jesus heard it, he answered him, saying, Fear not: believe only, and she shall be made whole. And when he came into the house, he suffered no man to go in, save Peter, and James, and John, and the father and the mother of the maiden. And all wept, and bewailed her: but he said, Weep not; she is not dead, but sleepeth. And they laughed him to scorn, knowing that she was dead. And he put them all out, and took her by the hand, and called, saying, Maid, arise.*

Luke 8:49-54

The last time I taught this material, the Lord had the account of Jairus read in the worship portion of the meeting for two weeks in a row. I couldn't see any connection to anything I was teaching on those particular evenings. Finally I realized that it was confirming the truth about *"they say."*

To recap the account at Jairus' house:

Grief had already settled on the onlookers. The situation seemed hopeless to them. "Don't waste your time; don't waste the Master's time," they said. But what did *Jesus* say, and do?

1. He said "Fear not, only believe!" In other words, do not be put off, by the circumstances – there is still hope. Jesus is greater than the observable circumstances or symptoms, even death!

2. Next, "He put them all out!" (Mark 5:40) Jesus put out all those who did not have faith, those who want to tell us that nothing can be done, and those who ridicule us for saying there is still hope. They actually laughed at Jesus, when He proclaimed that there was still hope for the girl to be made whole. They had no faith; their entire focus was on death, and this caused death to their faith. Notice also that *Jesus artificially raised the level of faith in that dead girl's room*, by limiting those allowed entrance. He limited the access to the girl's parents, and His three trusted disciples: all non-believers were excluded! He raised the level of faith by eliminating the nay-sayers and their negative faith.

Jairus' account gives a scriptural basis for refusing to believe what *"they say,"* – *"they,"* the unbelieving majority. We're not to believe what *they say*, (based upon our role model, Jesus) even, if they are right and stating valid observable facts, such as they did when they said "The girl is dead." Faith is the evidence of things *not yet seen.*

If what *they say* conflicts with, or opposes, either the

Word of God, the words of your faith, or the words of Jesus, then we are not to fall into the trap of believing what *they say*.

* * *

If you have seen blocks in this chapter that you feel relate to you, you might start your prayer:

*Thank You, Lord Jesus for showing me that I cannot alway trust what man may say to me. I thankYou for being the personification of the Spirit of Truth and that I can always believe in You, and in Your Word.*

* * *

These truths, which cause us to distrust the reports made by man, also hold true with regard to those who use Paul's "thorn" as an objection to healing.

# Chapter 7

# "What about
Paul's Thorn in the Flesh?"

A misunderstanding of Paul's thorn in the flesh is one of the most important theological blocks to healing that we encounter. It is a crucial question. "What about Paul's thorn?"

When speaking to an audience on healing, as I have often done, invariably there will be someone in the back row who will stand up, shake his fist, and shout: "Yes, but what about *Paul's thorn*?"

Paul's thorn is a pivotal issue that needs to be confronted for two reasons. First of all, it is a crucially important theological question, because the opponents of healing use it as the primary scriptural basis for an attempt to refute or deny healing. It also calls into question the consistency of the will of God as expressed in Scripture.

Secondly, it is an issue that is important to an individual seeking healing, because it can be an obstacle to faith. To think that even one man was refused healing through the ministry of Jesus and His early church would leave a huge question as to whether God's healing promises are for all, especially when that man was Paul!

For example, how could I, as a terminal cancer patient back in 1970, expect God to heal *me* if He didn't choose to heal *one of the King's own men*? If healing wasn't for Paul, then healing obviously wasn't intended for everyone. And therefore it probably wasn't for me, and it probably wasn't for you.

Those who teach that the Body of Christ today should be subject to sickness and disease will usually cite the case of Paul's thorn as a justification for their view. Therefore, we must at some point honestly face the question: *"Was Paul's thorn a sickness?"*

This mystery surounding Paul is described in the New Testament with the use of a figure of speech: "a thorn in the flesh." Most authorities admit that there is no justification or Scriptural evidence for this phrase to be interpreted as a sickness. What does the Scripture have to say?

## Paul's Thorn Introduced

*And lest I should be exalted above measure through the abundance of the revelations, there was given to me **a thorn in the flesh**, the messenger of Satan to buffet me, lest I should be exalted above measure.*
2 Cor. 12:7

That Paul had something which he described as "a thorn in the flesh" is indisputable. However, what the thorn actually was has been open to much debate. For me, personally, when I had cancer, Paul's "thorn" was a major stumbling block. How could I, as a mere nobody, expect God to heal me, if for some reason one of the greatest men of the New Testament era was not eligible for healing? If I was ever to be healed, I had to settle for myself the issue of whether or not Paul's thorn was a physical affliction.

What was to come was an abundance of revelation, grounded in the principle that the Word of God never contradicts itself. Over the years, the Lord has provided the following principles to better understand the thorn that plagued Paul. There have been so many revelations on this matter, that they now number *over twenty*. Many of these principles of Godly wisdom are numbered below:

## What Was Paul's Thorn?

### 1. *The Bible Never Contradicts*

Logically, I could not understand how this thorn could be a physical affliction. If it indeed was, it stood in contradiction to every other healing promise in Scripture, as well as all the experiences of healing I had discovered in the Scriptures. It also stood in contradiction to the demonstrated will of God.

### 2. *Where Was The Evidence That Paul Was Sick?*

It was apparent to me that Paul did not act sick. He ministered extensively and for extended periods. He made long and arduous journeys: not traveling in air-conditioned limousines like some modern evangelists, but rather traveling on donkey back, or on foot, or aboard ship (three of which wound up shipwrecked).

### 3. *Paul Was Not Reticent to List All His Hardships*

I noticed that Paul was not in the least bit shy about citing the hardships which he endured in the Lord's service. He lists twenty-eight of them just in the eleventh chapter of Second Corinthians (vs. 23-28) and more than a dozen more in Acts, and others elsewhere in Corinthians. Yet nowhere, in any of those listings, does he mention the inconvenience of a sickness, nor specify a physical ailment! Contrast that with the fact that almost every denomination and non-Charismatic author assures us, when discussing healing, that the Apostle Paul had a debilitating physical infirmity.

## 4. *The Law Of Large Numbers*

Scripture is very logical. To attempt to refute all of the specific promises for healing and physical blessings found in the Scripture with one, solitary, unspecified "thorn" of Paul is very poor logic. It is improper logic to take that one unknown (even those who stress it as an objection to healing acknowledge it to be uncertain in nature) and attempt thereby to negate all the specific statements of truth and Biblical promises that conflict with it. Take for instance the hundreds of promises made by God concerning healing and provision for His faithful people.

## 5. *The Law Of First Mention*

One of the premises of Scriptural interpretation is the Law of First Mention, which states that once Scripture attaches a symbolic meaning or definition to a word, it stands unless there clearly is a new definition or meaning given to that word or symbol.

In natural and normal usage, we can all agree, a thorn is a symbol of an external problem: something encountered causing pricking pain from without, *not from within*. Without exception, the literal use of the word "thorn" is just that, a thorn. Remember the crown of thorns; the long spike-like thorns about two inches long, which composed the crown that was crushed down upon the head of our Lord? However, Paul's thorn is figurative, and so we must look to the first figurative mention of "thorn" in the Old Testament.

## 6. *What Is A Figurative "Thorn" In The Bible?*

A basic question is, **"What is a thorn in Scriptural usage?"** When used figuratively, the word "thorn" is used in *only one way*.

There is no place in Scripture where the figurative use of thorn is changed, and therefore we can rely on the basis

102

of the Law of First Mention. I would submit to you that the only figurative use of thorn is when it relates to *an enemy* or *enemy personality*. Furthermore, the word "thorn" is never used figuratively in Scripture to describe an inanimate thing, such as a sickness!

What then specifically is a symbolic "thorn" in Scripture? The symbolic meaning for a thorn is first demonstrated in the Book of Numbers, and refers to the archenemy of the Israelites, the Canaanites. I quote the entire verse:

> *But if ye will not drive out the inhabitants of the land from before you; then it shall come to pass, that those which ye let remain of them shall be pricks in your eyes, and **thorns in your sides**, and shall vex you in the land wherein ye dwell.* Num. 33:55

This same symbolic usage occurs again in Judges 2:3 with the identical meaning. And it appears again in II Samuel and Isaiah 33:12, but again, the clear symbolic meaning refers to men (enemies) as "thorns."

> *But the sons of Belial shall be all of them as **thorns** thrust away, because they cannot be taken with hands:*
> 2 Sam. 23:6

> *And the people shall be as the burnings of lime: **as thorns** cut up shall they be burned in the fire.*
> Isa. 33:12

So there is absolutely *no Scriptural precedent* for interpreting Paul's thorn in the flesh as a physical affliction.

### What Was the Function of His Thorn?
What was the nature of the thorn that Paul had and how did it function?

103

By his own testimony, as a man of God, it was a "messenger from Satan" sent to buffet him.

> ...*there was given to me **a thorn in the flesh**, the messenger of Satan to buffet me, lest I should be exalted above measure.*
>
> 2 Cor. 12:7

Paul tells us three things in that brief phrase – what it was, from whence it came, and for what purpose it was given. Simply put, (1) it was a *messenger*, (2) it was *from Satan*, (3), and it was sent *to buffet him*. Let's consider each of those points in turn.

### 7. *How Did Paul Explain His Thorn?*

First, Paul himself explains his thorn in the flesh as being a (or *the*) *messenger of Satan*, which had been sent to buffet him. The Greek word translated as messenger is *aggelos*, or *ángelos*, the male gender form of the word which means "angel" or "messenger." A*ggelos* is the Greek word from which we get our word "angel."

In all but seven of the one hundred eighty-one occurrences of the word *aggelos* in the Scripture, this word is used to signify a male angel. In most of the other occurrences it is translated either as "him" or "he," and in the instance of Paul's thorn it is translated as "messenger."

### 8. *Who Was The Source Of The Thorn?*

The second point we want to note is that Satan is stated to be the source. Since it was a messenger sent from Satan, as Paul states, it could not be an angel sent by God! Rather, it had to be a demonic messenger sent to buffet Paul.

**A messenger from Satan.** How can the evangelical world turn this around to try to prove that sickness is from God? This makes no sense. Clearly the Word of God says the thorn is from Satan.

## 9. *What Does it Mean to Be "Buffeted"?*

The third point deals with the effect of the thorn. What does "*to buffet me*" mean, literally or symbolically? This is rendered from the Greek word *kolaphizo* meaning "to rap with the fist" or "to buffet." The meaning connotes a repeated hitting with the fist, in the sense that a prize fighter might be pummeled upon, or as waves which continually buffet the hull of a ship. But notice that both actions are external, and originate *from without*, not *from within*, as might be the case with a sickness or disease.

The first occurrence in the New Testament of the word "buffet" occurs in Matthew 26:67 where it is used to describe the soldiers hitting Jesus during his trial before the Sanhedrin and Caiaphas, which again illustrates an external action.

> *And some began to spit on him, and to cover his face, and **to buffet him**, and to say unto him, Prophesy: and the servants did strike him with the palms of their hands.* Mark 14:65

> *Then did they spit in his face, and **buffeted him**; and others smote him with the palms of their hands.* Mat. 26:67

They "buffeted" the Lord Jesus Christ. How did they buffet Him? They hit Him blow, after blow, after blow. They delivered repeated fists until His face was so marred beyond recognition that he did not even look like a man. (Isa. 52:14)

Note, we are not promised deliverance from all forms of **persecution** as we are from **sickness**. Paul tells us we will go through tribulation of some form, and this requires perseverance which in turn produces character and hope (Rom. 5:3). Perhaps this gives a clue as to the nature of Paul's thorn.

The Apostle Peter also writes of some receiving a "beating" for their own faults, and he uses the same word Paul uses for "buffeted" (1 Pet. 2:20). Again, this implies that the buffeting comes from an external source. Certainly Paul's enemies buffeted him with persecution repeatedly, and it was from a force outside his body.

Perhaps the most conclusive proof of Paul's usage of the term "buffet," which I believe confirms our interpretation of this aspect of his "thorn," is found in 1st Corinthians 4:11, where he uses this precise word to say:

> Even unto this present hour we both hunger, and thirst, and are naked, and **are buffeted**, and have no certain dwelling place; 1 Cor. 4:11

Finally, Paul gives an enumeration of the other "buffetings" he endured. And these are evidence of still more activities or work of the *angelos.* In 2nd Corinthians 11, starting at the 23rd verse, notice some of the other buffetings that he endured. Again, there is no mention of a sickness in the list.

> Are they ministers of Christ? (I speak as a fool) I am more; in **labours more abundant**, in **stripes above measure**, in **prisons more frequent**, in **deaths oft**. Of the Jews **five times received I forty stripes save one. Thrice was I beaten with rods, once was I stoned, thrice I suffered shipwreck, a night and a day** I have been **in the deep;** In **journeyings often**, in **perils of waters**, in **perils of robbers**, in **perils by mine own countrymen**, in **perils by the heathen**, in **perils in the**

*city, in perils in the wilderness, in perils in the sea, in*
*perils among false brethren; In weariness and pain-*
*fulness, in watchings often, in hunger and thirst, in*
*fastings often, in cold and nakedness.* *Beside those*
*things that are without, that which cometh upon me*
*daily, the care of all the churches.* *Who is weak, and*
*I am not weak? who is offended, and I burn not? If I*
*must needs glory, I will glory of the things which con-*
*cern mine infirmities* [feebleness, weaknesses]. *The*
*God and Father of our Lord Jesus Christ, which is*
*blessed for evermore, knoweth that I lie not. In Dam-*
*ascus the governor under Aretas the king kept the city*
*of the Damascenes with a garrison, desirous to ap-*
*prehend me: And through a window in a basket was*
*I let down by the wall, and escaped his hands.*

2 Cor. 11:23-33

### Why Did Paul Have His Thorn?

This brings us to the question of why Paul had this thorn in the first place.

## 10. *The Wonders He Has Seen*

Paul himself twice tells us the reason for which he had his "thorn," not merely once, but two times in verse seven. It was given "*lest I should be exalted above measure,*" or in other words, due to the abundance of the revelations which he had received. The thorn was given to him to prevent him from becoming exalted or prideful, from becoming puffed up over the magnitude of the revelation which he had been granted. Paul was allowed to see God more clearly perhaps than any human before or since.

I will often ask those who tell me their sickness is just their personal "thorn to bear," to share with me some of the abundance of the revelations that they have received which necessitated them having a thorn. This, after all, appears to be the Scriptural basis for having a thorn.

Paul indicated that the value of the "thorn," and the reason for its removal being delayed, was *lest he be exalted above measure*. The literal meaning is "lest I exalt myself" or "become haughty." Paul might easily have become prideful, because of his revelations. Take for instance revelations acquired upon being caught up into the third heaven and learning things which he could not reveal, and having Jesus appear personally to Him (Acts 9:17,26:16).

Consider Paul's own testimony in context regarding his thorn, as recorded in 2nd Corinthians 12:1

> *It is not expedient for me doubtless to glory. I will come to visions and revelations of the Lord. I knew a man in Christ above fourteen years ago, (whether in the body, I cannot tell; or whether out of the body, I cannot tell: God knoweth;) such an one caught up to the third heaven.*               2 Cor. 12:1-2

Paul here is apparently describing himself, having been caught up to the third heaven. Thus, the context in which the "thorn" is set is Paul's having been caught up into Heaven and receiving great revelations.

> *And I knew such a man, (whether in the body, or out of the body, I cannot tell: God knoweth;) How that he was caught up into paradise, and heard unspeakable words, which it is not lawful for a man to utter.*               2 Cor. 12:3-4

Paul heard things and saw things so glorious that he could not even legally speak of them unto men.

> *For though I would desire to glory, I shall not be a fool; for I will say the truth: but now I forbear, lest any man should think of me above that which he seeth*

*me to be, or that he heareth of me. And lest I should be exalted above measure through the abundance of the revelations, there was given to me a thorn in the flesh, the messenger of Satan to buffet me, lest I should be exalted above measure.* 2 Cor. 12:6-7

Now what revelations were these? The revelations of what he had seen – "visions and revelations of *the Lord*."

## Was Paul Happy about Having His Thorn?

No, obviously, he was not. He had prayed three times for it to be removed. In verse eight we read, "For this thing I besought the Lord thrice," three times, "that *it* might depart." Many other translations render the gender of "it," as "he," as in "that he might depart." For example the *Rotherham* reads, "that *he* might depart from me."

*For this thing I besought the Lord thrice, that it might depart from me. And he said unto me, My grace is sufficient for thee: for my strength is made perfect in weakness. Most gladly therefore will I rather glory in my infirmities* [lit. in "feebleness", "weaknesses"], *that the power of Christ may rest upon me. Therefore I take pleasure in infirmities* ["feebleness," "weaknesses"], *in reproaches, in necessities, in persecutions, in distresses for Christ's sake: for when I am weak, then am I strong. I am become a fool in glorying; ye have compelled me: for I ought to have been commended of you: for in nothing am I behind the very chiefest apostles, though I be nothing. Truly the signs of an apostle were wrought among you in all patience, in signs, and wonders, and mighty deeds.*
2 Cor. 12:8-12

Notice in the above passage, that Paul lists "infirmities" along with reproaches or "insults," necessities or "constraints" – from a root meaning arm-bending, persecutions, and distresses. That is, he is listing **external opposing influences**. Even the translation of the Greek word into English creates confusion. The NIV Version uses "weaknesses" instead of "infirmities," a far better translation

That Paul continued to minister in spite of his "thorn," in the strength and grace of the Lord is evident. However, this neither proves that the thorn was a physical affliction, nor does it justify denying the Lord's power or will to heal. "Let the weak say I am strong," God admonished through Joel (3:10), and that is exactly what Paul does – glorifying God through the strength which He provides in spite of his own weakness.

The opponents of healing place great emphasis upon grace in the above passage, and say that Paul didn't need healing for his body (thorn), because he received grace instead. They err again. **Grace** is something given by God for an inner condition – for a soul problem; it is for inner strength. We are strengthened in our inner man by the grace of God. **Healing** is for the *outer man*. If we may draw the distinction, the one is for the soul, the other is for the body. By grace we are saved; we are called by grace; and grace is for an inner condition rather than a outer, bodily condition.

## Was Paul's Problem Eye Trouble?

11. *Did Paul Need An Ophthalmologist?*

Many today believe and teach that Paul had ophthalmia, a debilitating disease of the eyes still commonly found among beggars in areas like the Middle East. Many Bibles even have a footnote which scholars have written, and many commentaries state without any equivocation, that Paul's problem was eye trouble – that Paul had ophthalmia! This disease affects the sight, causes extreme weakness and a pussy discharge from the eyes. Those who expound this theory cite as proof two statements made by Paul in Galatians. Let's analyze both of the statements and permit Scripture to explain itself, and in doing so, do away with all their arguments against healing.

Paul speaks of the weakness in his flesh, which he had when he first came to the Galatians, probably shortly after his stoning.

> *Ye know how through infirmity of the flesh I preached the gospel unto you at the first. And my temptation which was in my flesh ye despised not, nor rejected; but received me as an angel of God, even as Christ Jesus. Where is then the blessedness you spake of where I bear you record that if it had been possible you would have plucked out your own eyes and had given them to me."*  Gal. 4:13-15

He speaks of people "plucking out their eyes." The Galatians had used a figure of speech, and Paul repeats it, in order to give an indication of the sincerity and the depth of their emotion and feeling for him. Even if Paul were blind in both eyes, he would have only needed *two* eyes. Had it been possible to get them, he wouldn't have needed the whole group to have plucked out their eyes and given them to him. This expression is obviously similar to one we use when we say, "He would have given his right arm for me."

The second statement of opposition given by the scholars is:

> *Ye see how **large** a letter I have written unto you with **mine own hand**.*  Gal. 6:11

The opponents of healing rather circuitously interpret

this to mean that Paul had eye trouble, and for that reason was forced to write in large letters in order to be able to see them! This, they suppose, confirms their dubious assumption that his sight was impaired. The fallacy in this reasoning is evident in that the word translated "large" connotes quantity and means "how much," rather than "how large in size." Several scholars believe that the reason Paul added this observation was that he himself wrote this letter in his own handwriting as the last phrase indicates, and did not on this occasion have the luxury of dictating it either to Luke, or one of his earlier assistants. This clearly has nothing to do with eye trouble. *Even if he had employed "large" letters, could it not have been for emphasis sake?* This would be the more obvious conclusion.

This, by the way, is the same Paul who wrote 1st Corinthians 12, teaching on the gifts of the Spirit and especially on the gifts of healing!

## 12. *On The Sickness In The Corinthian Church*

Another logical consideration worth noting is that Paul wrote a letter to the Corinthians in which he told them that the reason for many of the Corinthians becoming sick, and many of them dying, was that they had not properly observed the Lord's Supper.

> *For he that eateth and drinketh unworthily, eateth and drinketh damnation to himself, not discerning the Lord's body. For this cause many are **weak and sickly** among you, and many sleep.*     1 Cor. 11:29-30

He was far too logical to have written what we have just read, if, indeed, he were himself ill.

Paul did not accept the fact of sickness within the church as normal, nor as a source of glory for God. Rather, he admonished the Corinthians for permitting the condition to exist. At the outset of man's existence, Adam also ate unworthily, not in obedience, and gave sickness entry to the human race. Paul's clear expectation was that to partake of Christ's body was to partake of His life and health; expecting it to be a quickening experience. To eat of it "unworthily," he teaches, was, like Adam, to eat unto death.

I suggest to you that if we had been in Corinth and received such a letter from a sick and afflicted Paul, we would have fired a letter right back to him asking what it was that he had failed to observe, which resulted in his own sickness! If Paul had been sick himself, how could he have criticized others for being sick?

### 13. *The Absurdity Of The Ophthalmia Proposition*

Had Paul indeed been plagued with ophthalmia, how could he have continued such a strenuous lifestyle? Paul preached all day and made tents at night to support himself. (Incidentally, sewing requires reasonably good eyesight.) We read in Acts that he lived for a time with Aquila and Priscilla because they shared the same craft.

> *And because he was of the same craft, he abode with them, and* **wrought***: for by their occupation they were* **tentmakers***.* Acts 18:3

Paul was self-supporting. Rather than being an object of ministry and care for the churches, Paul instead worked long and hard to support himself, and his fellow-laborers...

> *I have coveted no man's silver, or gold, or apparel. Yea, ye yourselves know, that **these hands have ministered unto my necessities**, and to them that were with me.* Acts 20:33-34

Paul own testimony was, in part, that he labored more abundantly than all the other Apostles...

> ...*but I laboured more abundantly than they all:* yet not I, but the grace of God which was with me.
>
> 1 Cor. 15:10

Paul could not have been sick and accomplished all that he did. He appears to have been the most traveled of all the disciples or Apostles.

### 15. *Paul's Healing Was Complete*

To me, implying that Paul had eye trouble borders on blasphemy. You will recall that Paul was blinded on the road to Damascus, but then God remedied his sight problem by sending Ananias to lay his hands on him. His sight was then restored, not partially but fully.

> And Ananias went his way, and entered into the house; and putting his hands on him said, Brother Saul, the Lord, even Jesus, that appeared unto thee in the way as thou camest, hath sent me, that **thou mightest receive thy sight**, and be filled with the Holy Ghost. And immediately there fell from his eyes as it had been scales: and **he received sight** forthwith, and arose, and was baptized.           Acts 9:17-18

If Paul were nearly blind, as some would have us believe, he did not consider his blindness 'a blessing in disguise,' because he thrice prayed for it to be removed from him. Further, he cast blindness upon the false prophet and sorcerer, Elymas–Bar-Jesus, (Acts 13:8) as a **curse.**

### 16. *Testing The Fruit*

To apply the "fruit" test to Paul's thorn: what was the

fruit of Paul's thorn? Did it impair his ministry? Did it leave Paul in doubt as to God's will regarding healing, as the modern interpretation of it does? I think not: Paul's ministry was exceptional, and was certainly filled with miracles of healing. Healings followed Paul's ministry from beginning to end, for individuals as well as groups.

> *And it came to pass, that the father of Publius lay sick of a fever and of a bloody flux* [hemorrhage]: *to whom Paul entered in, and prayed, and laid his hands on him, and* **healed him**. *So when this was done,* **others also**, *which had diseases in the island,* **came, and were healed:**                                                    Acts 28:8-9

Not only was Paul not in doubt about the Lord's will to heal, but of him alone it is recorded that God worked special miracles of healing and deliverance through his hands.

> *And God wrought* **special miracles by the hands of Paul**: *So that from his body were brought unto the sick handkerchiefs or aprons, and the diseases departed from them, and the evil spirits went out of them.*
>                                                    Acts 19:11-12

## 17. *Paul's Life Was Full Of Healing*

I believe that Paul knew, experientially, the healing power of God in answer to the prayers of believers. When he was stoned, apparently to death, his "executioners" carried him out of the city and discarded his body (Acts 14:19). Afterwards, the believers gathered around him, forming the first recorded "prayer-circle." The disciples prayed for Paul and God responded, raising him back to life. Paul was so completely restored that he could continue his journey the following day!

*And there came thither certain Jews from Antioch and Iconium, who persuaded the people, and, having **stoned Paul**, drew him out of the city, **supposing he had been dead.** Howbeit, as the disciples stood round about him, he rose up, and came into the city: and the next day he departed with Barnabas to Derbe.*

Acts 14:19-20

Consider the fact that the men who stoned Paul were not amateurs; they had done this before. Some have interpreted this passage as if they had made a mistake, misdiagnosing Paul as being dead. I don't think they misdiagnosed his condition at all; I think Paul *was* dead. They carried him outside the town, probably half an hour's walk and threw him on the city's garbage dump after stoning him.

Conceivably, someone could have misdiagnosed his condition after he had been stoned, and walked away leaving him for dead. It is also possible for someone to fake death for a moment or two. However, when the executioners pick up a body, and carry it for half an hour, no matter how strong the individual may be, or how desirous of pretending to be dead, he is going to groan, moan, or breathe noticeably. It would be detected by those who were carrying him.

Recognize also that "being stoned" is not merely somebody hitting you over the head once with a stone. A group of people stand around the victim and hurl fairly large size stones, until he is literally crushed and torn apart; pummeled to death.

## In The End, Hypocrisy

18. *Paul Ministered Until The End*

Finally, Paul reported at the end of his life ...

*For I am now ready to be offered, and the time of my departure is at hand. I have fought a good fight, **I have finished my course**, I have kept the faith:*

2 Tim. 4:6-7

Paul completed his appointed tasks, so that at the end of his life he could truthfully say, "I have *finished* (completed) my course." He was not forced to cut short, or in any way curtail, his ministry efforts due to sickness or disease. Paul stands as a strong proponent of the Gospel of healing. And, I believe, he would be offended to know that his words have been twisted into an argument against the very ministry of healing and miracles which God so abundantly manifested through him.

Is it not strange that those who teach that Paul's thorn in the flesh was a physical sickness use their teachings to refute the very type of ministry which Paul had – a miraculous healing ministry!

Paul, by his own testimony, and as Scripture confirms, worked miracles, signs and wonders and mighty deeds, *and* did all the works of an apostle. Again, is it not strange, since "faith cometh by hearing," that those who teach the opposite of our interpretation of Paul's thorn actually **refute** and **destroy faith!**

Paul prayed for his condition to be removed. Those who argue that Paul's thorn was a sickness hypocritically would say "Go to the doctor for it." Paul knew why he had his condition, while they do not seem to care why the condition exists, if it can be removed by a doctor.

Paul built faith in his hearers to be healed; his opponents do not, neither do they seek healing themselves. Paul had a supernatural ministry, they do not. Paul was used in special miracles, they are not. Paul gloried in his weakness, do they? Those who have been taught that Paul's thorn was a physical sickness, do they really glory in their sickness and consider it a blessing? I submit to you that they do not. If they did, they would be praying, Lord, send more, make me sicker. But obviously they do not, because when they become sick, they immediately run to a physician to try to take away that "blessing of sickness" and to be made whole.

### What, Then, Might Paul's Thorn Have Been?

Based upon the fact that the scriptural usage of thorn figuratively means "an enemy," or "one who persecutes," I believe, that his "thorn" represents wicked human personalities employed as Satan's agents against God's will. I think it's very logical to assume that he was making reference to his Jewish enemies, or the *aggelos* behind those who followed him about in order to persecute him.

You will recall Paul himself had been a religious zealot, a Christian hater, a persecutor, and killer of Christians. It is very possible that there were other Jews just like him ("perils of *my own countrymen*") who resented the fact that they felt he had departed from the faith as a Jew by becoming "a Christian." His life was an affront to the Jews, and the religious Jewish zealots hated him as a heretic and traitor. No doubt, there were those who chose to follow him about and to persecute him.

There was, for instance, one group of more than 40 men who swore an oath that they would neither eat nor drink until they had killed Paul. (Acts 23:13) There is no other way to explain such intense evil, other than **satanically inspired hatred**.

Again, Paul had just raised the crippled man at Lystra, as recorded in Acts 14:8, *"who was impotent in his feet, a cripple from his mother's womb, who had never walked. The same heard Paul speaking, steadfastly beholding Paul, Paul perceiving that he had faith to be healed, told him to stand up, and he was healed."*

Now the people of the city of Lystra were so astounded by the fantastic miracle of this man, crippled from birth, being raised and healed, that they brought animals to sacrifice to Paul and to Barnabas.

Consider the situation: here is a crowd of people so impressed with Paul and Barnabas, that they wanted to sacrifice to them. Yet what happens almost immediately? A group of Jews arrive from Antioch, and persuade the people to try to stone the pair to death. What a transition: one minute the crowd wants to hang garlands around their necks, kill the fatted calf, and slaughter animals to sacrifice to them, because they think they are gods; the next, the persecuting Jewish zealots convince them to stone Paul and Barnabas. This appears to be satanically inspired hatred, to say the least.

I would certainly consider this to be persecution. Paul was an expert, unfortunately, on persecution and tribulation. And he had his share of messengers, or demonic angels (*aggelos*), who buffeted him and his work.

Jesus spoke to Paul at his conversion and warned him about the "great things he would have to suffer for the gospel's sake;" that he was a chosen vessel; and that he was going to have to suffer for the sake of Jesus' name (Acts 9:15-16).

### Why Didn't Paul Have Doubts about God's Will to Heal?

If Paul, himself, were incurably sick, as the opponents of healing today would like us to believe, certainly he would have had to have doubts about the will of God to heal. **But he didn't.** Consider just one of numerous statements that Paul made.

*But if the Spirit of him that raised up Jesus from the dead dwell in you, he that raised up Christ from the dead shall also **quicken your mortal bodies** by his Spirit that dwelleth in you.*                    Rom. 8:11

"Quickening your mortal bodies," means making them alive. This is going to occur because of the current indwelling of the Holy Spirit ("the Spirit *that dwelleth*," meaning in the present). God is going to heal, and make alive, your mortal bodies. That's the message that Paul repeatedly shares, throughout his letters. Paul did not attempt to explain away sickness, he instead cast it out! And he's the only man recorded in the New Testament to have been employed in special miracles.

Paul, the apostle, was not only the most gifted Apostle, but also had more revelations than any of the other apostles, gave more teaching on healing than any of the other apostles, and was the most persecuted of all the apostles. Admittedly we only have his testimony to that fact, but I think we can assume that the Holy Spirit has given an accurate commentary upon the conditions in the early church, and that Paul, indeed, was the most persecuted of all the apostles.

If you have seen blocks in this chapter that you feel relate to you, you might start your prayer:

*Lord, please forgive me for being misled concerning Paul's thorn. I thank you for revealing scriptural truths to me.*

\* \* \*

The next most commonly raised objection or block to healing is the issue of Job.

# Chapter 8

# "What about Job's Ordeal?"

Another major healing block which I had to confront was...the issue of "But what about Job?"

The erroneous beliefs concerning the account of Job are a further example of the problem of *"they say"* covered in Chapter Six. Never allow yourself to believe something outside of the Word of God. In the same sense do not allow yourself to miss the crucial healing issues in the Book of Job, for there is really an underlying message of healing contained within his story. Notice:

(1) God had a hedge of protection around Job and all his possessions (1:10).

(2) God did not set Satan on Job as we have been taught. He literally observed a fact, that "Hath thou [Satan] considered [literally *suwm leb* "set your heart, or mind, on"] my servant Job?"

(3) God *did not give* Satan permission to afflict Job. Rather He merely stated the fact that, *"all that he hath is* [already] *in thy power."* God then limited Satan's sphere of activity, stating, *"Only upon himself put not forth thine hand."* (1:12)

(4) Satan's goal and desire was to kill Job (2:4-6). Apparently Job was not only a reminder to him of his own disobedience, but also proof that mere human beings could

do what he as a supernatural being had been unable to accomplish, remain faithful to God.

(5) Satan attempted to get God to afflict Job, but *God would not!*

(6) Satan is a liar, and seeks to place the blame on God by suggesting, *"You* afflict him," but this was not to be the case. It was *Satan* who afflicted Job, and not God.

> *So went **Satan** forth from the presence of the LORD, and **smote Job** with sore boils from the sole of his foot unto his crown.* (2:7)

(See seven proofs of Satanic Source of sickness in Chapter Three.)

(7) The world has always bought into Satan's lie, that God seeks to destroy man (through natural disasters, "acts of God"). For instance, the messenger reported, "the fire *of God* has destroyed your flock" (1:16).

(8) Even Job believed the lie, and assumed that it was "the Lord" who "hath taken away."

(9) Job's affliction was an expression of the will of Satan, not of God's will.

(10) Job's affliction pleased Satan, and not God.

(11) Scripture refers to Job's condition as *captivity* (42:10; cf 2 Tim. 2:26)

(12) Scripture records that after Job came to really know the Lord (42:5-6), that he repented, and prayed for his friends, and that then the Lord blessed Job with twice the

possessions that he had formerly, and restored to him seven sons and three daughters.

> *And the LORD turned the captivity of Job, when he prayed for his friends: also the LORD gave Job twice as much as he had before. So the LORD blessed the latter end of Job more than his beginning: for he had fourteen thousand sheep, and six thousand camels, and a thousand yoke of oxen, and a thousand she asses. He had also seven sons and three daughters.*
>
> Job 42:10-13

(13) The world has mistakenly assumed that God gave Satan permission to attack Job. To restate and underscore a very crucial point previously made: Satan did not need God's permission to be a devil; he *already was* the Devil. God merely stated *the fact* that Job *was in* Satan's power.

> *And the Lord said unto Satan, Behold, he is in thine hand...* (2:6a)

This was a result of Adam having forfeited to Satan the dominion which God granted to him at the beginning, which explains how Satan became 'god of this world' (2 Cor. 4:4). Thus, Satan has a legal right to function in this present world. However, even with the legal right of Satan over Job, note that God, in His mercy and faithfulness, placed a limitation upon Satan's power.

> *Behold, **all that he hath is in thy power**; only upon himself put not forth thine hand.* (1:12)

(14) God actually prevented the Devil from killing Job as he wished to do.

123

*...but save his life.* (2:6b)

Many have mistakenly assumed that Job was without sin, because God said he was "perfect." Job was not sinless, only Jesus Christ has that distinction among men born of women. Rather he was morally mature and complete. God called him "perfect" because he feared God and eschewed evil. (Job 1:1) Note the words of Jesus on perfection:

*Be ye therefore perfect, even as your Father which is in heaven is perfect* [lit. mature, complete].

Mat. 5:48

Clearly, we are not sinlessly perfect either, but our goal is perfection: to be like our Father in Heaven. We strive to emulate His characteristics, such as kindness which seems to be the point in Matthew's statement above. We are to study the Word and studiously seek that goal.

*That the man of God may be perfect, thoroughly furnished unto all good works.* 2 Tim. 3:17

### Flaws in Job's Character

To underscore this point, that Jesus Christ is the only man completely without sin in the history of the world, there were certain flaws in Job's character that are revealed in his story. Five of these merit our notice:

1. he had married an ungodly wife (2:9);

2. his children were out of order, with a tendency to curse God (1:5b),

3. self-righteousness (32:1),

124

4. and pride (33:9)

5. his faith was not perfect. For example he admits that, even though he was under God's protection, he feared. Note the following Scriptures:

*For the thing which **I greatly feared** is come upon me, and that which I was afraid of is come unto me.*
Job 3:25

*And, we know that fear is not from the Lord. For God hath not given us the spirit of fear...*    2 Tim. 1:7

Job like many men since, misinterpreted what happened to him. He erred, when he said, *"The Lord gave, and **the Lord** hath taken away"* (Job 1:21). It *was* the **Lord who gave**, but it was **Satan who took away**.

### Job, An Example of Divine Healing

Job is considered to be the oldest book in the Bible. It was apparently recorded before the Mosaic law, as there is no mention of it. Yet even in this case, Job was healed without the law and without a specific promise! Recognize also, that unlike today, salvation through grace was not available to Job, nor was the Name of Jesus, nor the Word of God, nor the Better Covenant, nor the presence and indwelling of the Holy Spirit, and yet he was healed! Therefore, how much greater should our expectation for healing be today!

Contrary to the traditions of man, Job is a healing book, **he was healed!** Futhermore, in the end, the Lord blessed him greatly. Formerly, he had been the richest man in the east (Job 1:3). At the conclusion of his story, Job wound up with twice the possessions he formerly had: each of his herds doubled; his sons and daughters were replaced with better ones – sons who were apparently obedient, and daughters who were the most beautiful in the land. In addition, not only was Job healed of his afflictions, but also blessed with long life – he lived 140 years longer, and was able to see four generations of his family prospering (Job 42:16, cf Psa. 91:16).

In the book of Job, we even see a foreshadowing of the principle given in James Chapter 5 of praying "for one another that ye may be healed." Because it was after he repented, confessed (42:6) and *prayed* for his three friends (42:10), that God healed Job. I often recommend that those people who are seeking God for a need, physical or otherwise, get actively involved in praying for others for similar needs. It shows a commitment of their wills and a submission to the teaching of James, to pray for one another..

Finally the Holy Spirit presents a summarizing commentary of the issues involving Job:

*Ye have heard of the patience of Job, and have seen the end of the Lord; that the Lord is very pitiful, and of tender mercy.*                                   James 5:11b


# What of Others in Scripture, Who Weren't Healed?

There are very few Godly individuals in the Scripture who were recorded as being sick. However, let's consider those in the New Testament. The two names we are most frequently challenged with, after Paul and Job, are Epaphroditus and Trophimus.

Regarding the latter, Paul wrote, *Trophimus have I left at Miletum sick.* (2 Tim 4:20b). Since Scripture is silent beyond that simple statement, we assume he was only incapacitated for short time. However, we are given more details on the case of Epaphroditus.

> *Yet I supposed it necessary to send to you Epaphroditus, my brother, and companion in labour, and fellowsoldier, but your messenger, and he that ministered to my wants. For he longed after you all, and was full of heaviness, because that ye had heard that **he had been sick**. For indeed **he was sick nigh unto death**: but God had mercy on him; and not on him only, but on me also, lest I should have sorrow upon sorrow.* Phil. 2:25-27

Then, Paul explains the reason that Epaphroditus had become ill almost to the point of death, before receiving the Lord's merciful healing touch. It was because he had been overworked. He was one of the earliest cases of ministerial "burn-out," wearing himself down in the process of earning funds with which to support Paul's ministry.

> *Because for the work of Christ he was nigh unto death, not regarding his life, to supply your lack of service toward me.* Phil. 2:30

Why did it take so long for Epaphroditus to recuperate? He required an extended period of convalescence because his body had become run down over a period of time. Usually in such cases, the body requires time to heal itself.

However, recover he did, because we read of his continued traveling ministry efforts, in visiting the Church at Phillipi and then returning to Paul with gifts from them (Phil.

2:25;4:18), in visiting the Church at Colasse (Col. 1:7;4:12), and finally imprisoned with Paul (Phile 1:23 ).

Again, simply by counting the sheer number of healing miracles in the Gospels, and then observing the continuation of this ministry through the disciples in Acts and elsewhere, we must conclude that healing was, and is, an intricate part of the message of Jesus Christ. And that it is consistent in every way with the mercy, love, compassion of God for His children. God is light, in Him there is no darkness at all.

Some proclaim that there must have been others whom Jesus did not heal, and often mention the name of Simon the Leper (Mat 26:6). Yet the exciting truth regarding Simon, is that He must have been healed by Jesus, which probably prompted him to invite Jesus to his home for a feast. Had he still been a leper, no one could have associated with him. Lepers you recall were required in Jewish society to avoid contact with others, and to cry "Leper" whenever anyone approached them.

*  *  *

If you have seen blocks in this chapter that you feel relate to you,  you might start your prayer::

*Lord  Jesus,  I thank you for all the healings of physical conditions that I see recorded in your Word.  I also thank You for showing me these truths from the Old Testament concerning Job which confirm your ongoing will to heal.*

*  *  *

"Okay, that's true for Paul and those men in the Bible, but what about me?  Do I have the necessary faith to be healed?"

# Chapter 9

# "Do I Have Enough Faith?"

### "How Much Faith Do I Need?"
The good news is that those who know Jesus as their Lord and Savior, and acknowledge the depth of His mercy and compassion, most likely already possess the faith that they need. Faith comes as a gift from Jesus, the Author and Finisher of our faith, and it cometh by hearing the word of God, as we learn in Romans.

> *So then faith cometh by hearing, and hearing by the*
> *word of God.*                                    Rom. 10:17

Paul amplifies our understanding of the required faith, by defining it:

> *But without faith it is impossible to please him: for he*
> *that cometh to God **must believe that he is**, and that*
> ***he is a rewarder of them** that diligently seek him.*
>                                                   Heb. 11:6

In order to have God-pleasing faith, we must first *Believe that He is*, i.e., that He exists, and second that *He is a rewarder* of those who seek Him diligently (search for Him, carefully). This means a belief that He is able to reward, or grant, those things we ask of Him. That doesn't seem too difficult for God, does it? You already believe that God exists, and that He can do things for you, or you wouldn't be praying to Him in the first place.

129

*...[God] is able to do exceeding abundantly above all that we ask or think, **according to the power that worketh in us.*** Eph. 3:20

Since God wills for all to be well and whole, there must, therefore, be a missing ingredient – *the power working in us* – which is often hindered by lack of faith, or other blocks. We need to learn how to remove those blocks, release that faith, and to cooperate with it.

People mistakenly assume that one must have a massive amount of faith in order to be healed. This is not supported by the message of the "mustard seed," nor by the evidence of healing in our 30 year ministry.

As an illustration of the above point: When I was healed of cancer, many people reacted by crediting me with possessing more faith than I did, saying, "You must have had a great deal of faith to have been healed of cancer and of all those other physical problems that you had." They erred. Great faith I did not have. Even if I did have great faith, the faith itself would have been a **gift**.

*For by grace are ye saved through **faith**; and that not of yourselves: it **is the gift of God***: Eph. 2:8

Faith for salvation is a gift, and I submit to you, that faith for healing is also often given as a gift.

All I could respond to those who flattered me, was that "Faith is a gift, lest any man boast." And today it is just as true for me now as it was then. The only difference between now and thirty years or more ago, is the fact that I have seen *thousands* of people healed in accordance with the will of God. Therefore, naturally my faith today should be much stronger than it was then, before I'd seen so many people miraculously healed. Seeing people healed is a powerful faith-builder. I was blessed with seeing many healings very early on, probably 200 in the first Kathryn Kuhlman service we attended. It's a tremendous faith-builder to see people being healed. And when we see God touch someone, it eradicates a lot of doubts.

## The Gift of A Healing

Whether I was given the gift of faith to be healed of cancer, or the gift of a healing from cancer, is a moot point, and merely a matter of semantics. In any event, the source of the gift in either case was God, and it was His power working in me, not my own.

For someone like me to have been the recipient of a gift, tells you nothing about me. For instance, had someone given me a brand new Cadillac as a gift, it would tell you nothing about me. Rather, it would speak volumes about the giver. He must have been unselfish, thoughtful, generous, wealthy, etc.

**The graciousness of the gift received only testifies to the goodness of the Giver of that gift.**

Regrettably, people often say...

## "I Have No Faith (To Be Healed)."

They are in error. They do have faith – they are expressing their faith when they say that they have *no faith*. And they are acting according to that faith, by not seeking healing, expecting there to not be faith available within them. This is **negative faith**, or unbelief, at work.

To make such a statement is an effective block against healing, because one acts upon that unbelief. The action, or resulting action in this case, is no action. To state the obvious, the one who believes he has no faith excludes himself from any kind of "faith" healing, refuses prayer to that end, and probably fails to expose himself to any type of ministry where healing is taking place. (Even so, on occasions, even such individual sometimes receive "mercy healings" from God without any faith involved.) Perhaps he feels ineligible, perhaps he fears being embarrassed by having his lack of faith exposed, or perhaps he simply doesn't want to be disappointed again. Positive faith and negative faith both lead to action of some kind.

God gave me a formula regarding faith during my own search for healing: *Faith, if it exists, will express itself in action!*

### "Do You Have A Fear of Being Disappointed?"

The fear of disappointment is an effective and common block. If you read the accounts of many of those who "haven't been healed," or accounts by some of the classic proponents of "God doesn't heal all..." or "God has a higher purpose in affliction," you will usually find a point in their testimony, when they made a decision not to allow anyone else to lay hands on them, or to pray for their healing. This is because they "did not want to be *disappointed* again." That, incidentally, is a refusal to allow God to be sovereign – a refusal to allow Him to heal, when and how He so chooses. It also may be indicative of the problem of *giving up too soon.* And it is a sign of negative faith.

### "But I Don't Have Enough Faith To Be Healed."

We tend to hear this condemning statement whispered in our ear from an *internal* source. Somehow from within ourselves, the Devil will attack our minds with the thought that we don't have enough faith to be healed, and the thought that somehow it must take an awful lot of faith in order to get healed. He then tries to convince us, that since we haven't been healed, then, obviously, we are *deficient* in that needed faith. This is all part of his tactics and lies. Remember, he was a "liar and a murderer from the beginning."

## "You Don't Have Enough Faith"
## "You Have Too Little Faith"

This is an entirely different issue than the previous block. Before, it was an internal doubt concerning the level of one's faith. Here it is *external*, or outside criticism of one's faith. In this case, someone is either making a judgmental assessment of you, or attempting to minister healing to you, and in the process, making a critical statement. This person is ministering to you negatively, instead of positively.

We are told to encourage one another, to build each other up in faith (1 Thess. 5:11). This is not the intent of the above critical approach. It is really an attempt to place blame on the sick person, rather than the lack of ministry skills on behalf of the person making the accusation. This is a sign of an unrighteous spirit on behalf of the accuser, because we know there is an accuser of the brethren, and that it is not Jesus, but rather the devil.

I have already covered this issue in my book, *Three Kinds of Faith for Healing*, however some additional thoughts are warranted.

When someone else accuses you of having no faith, it is of no benefit to you and, in effect, ministers condemnation to you (which is not a ministry of the Holy Spirit). It is also a spoken curse. I have found myself on the receiving end of this kind of "ministry," and I can testify that it was of no value to me. When I do not have the faith to be healed, I am aware that I don't have faith. What I need is someone to tell me how to get some (or more) faith to support my search for healing. [For example, to increase faith one should: read the Scriptural accounts of healings (See Appendix) because " faith cometh by hearing (Rom. 10:17) read inspiring testimonies of others who have been healed, attend meetings where prayer is offered and healings are taking place, associate with positive people, who are "like-minded" about healing.]

I had a similar, yet even worse, experience years ago when someone told me "in love" that the reason I was not being healed was "because there was so much unconfessed sin in my life." Fortunately I had the presence of mind to respond, "Thank you for revealing that; now tell me what my sin is, so that I can confess it and repent of it." The "prophet" was suddenly speechless.

### Faith And Unbelief Are Often Both Present

Recognize that it is possible for both faith and doubt to exist in a person at the same time. I have encountered both often.

In Matthew 17, Jesus criticized His disciples for their inability to perform the deliverance and healing needed by the lunatic boy, and called them "faithless." Why was His criticism legitimate? (1) He had previously commissioned them in Matthew 10:1, specifically giving them *power to cast out unclean spirits.* (2) Their question as to why they could not cast out this specific spirit implied that they had been successful in casting out and healing all the other cases they had encountered. And finally, (3) Jesus' answer, important enough to be recorded in each of the first three Gospels, gives us an integral key: "*O faithless* ["disbelieving," "unbelieving"] *and perverse* ["turning away"] *generation, how long shall I be with you? how long shall I suffer you? bring him hither to me.*"

By analyzing the Greek words involved, we notice that it was actually not a lack of faith that He criticized, but a *willful* disbelief.

The Devil often tries to tell me that a particular individual isn't going to be healed when we pray for him or her, or that healing isn't going to work *this* time. We must ignore the doubts and believe our faith, and have faith in the Word. Like lifting weights to build muscles, we must exercise our faith in the Word and in the promises of God!

Another Scriptural proof that both can exist simultaneously is to be seen in the case of Jairus who cried out, *"Lord I believe; Help thou my unbelief."* We have all prayed that prayer with him at one time or another.

Faith and unbelief can both be in operation, and we must choose to believe, to go with the faith portion. I think of this process as a balancing scale, with belief on one side and unbelief on the other. The deciding factor will be the weight of our will added to one side or the other.

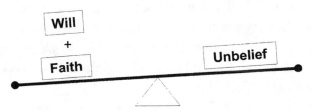

*The Difference Human Will Can Make*

These disciples had faith, but also had unbelief – perhaps due to seeing the demonic, suicidal manifestations in the boy as they prayed. I have often encountered similar situations, where the demons attempted to make the pending deliverance so unpleasant or difficult that either I, or the candidate, might become discouraged and give up before receiving the desired blessing.

The disciples had faith, but were also confronted by the observable symptoms causing doubt – they needed prayer and fasting to change themselves, and to rid themselves of doubt and disbelief. They were instructed to seek dominance over their own doubting wills, by fasting and prayer.

> *Howbeit this kind goeth not out but by **prayer and
> fasting**.*                                    Matt 17:21

### "Must I Study Healing To Get Healed?"

When you are ministering salvation to someone, and
ask them if they're saved, and they say, "I *hope* I'm saved,
or I *think maybe* I'm saved," you immediately experience
an inner check. You know that they do not fully know Jesus
as Savior – that they do not understand salvation, nor have
the confidence in the complete work of grace on the cross.

Likewise with regard to healing, some don't know Jesus
as Healer, or that He still heals, and others don't understand
healing. There is great value in studying the instances of
healing by Jesus in the Gospels, and meditating on these
acts of His will. Likewise, it is of great importance to study
the other healing promises in Scripture in order to know the
Lord's will on the matter. This is, after all, a Rock on which
we can stand. So I would naturally encourage all who are
sick to look to the Word of God.

However, I am not implying that you have to understand
everything about healing to get healed. Consider all those
unsaved people in the New Testament who were healed;
not one of those who received healing from Jesus, when He
walked the streets of Galilee in the flesh, had the opportunity
to accept Him as their Risen Savior. He had not yet died for
them! They simply came to Jesus with their needs and
received their healings (without having read books by
anyone). They were healed, sovereignly, without any prior
knowledge. They were healed *before* the cross, and they
were healed on the basis of an older covenant that was not
as good as the covenant that you and I possess. (Heb. 8:6).
Yet, even then, the power of God was sufficient to heal

everyone that came to Jesus – none were turned away, none were refused healing.

Today we're under a new and better covenant; "better" means it is stronger, and the promises are more sure. It contains better promises, because they're based on the blood of Jesus, because we are on this side of Calvary, and because we have access to all that was purchased there.

## Have You Boxed God In, or Out?

Another block we've encountered over the years of ministry is the problem of people putting God in a **faith box**. I remember one of the early meetings we attended was 'Camps Farthest Out,' held in Georgia. The speaker for that meeting was one of the leading faith teachers (now deceased). He happened to be a cripple, having had polio as a child. As such, he had one withered leg which was much shorter than the other. Normally when he was to speak at a convention or a conference, they would have him already at the podium standing on a step. To prevent the audience seeing him hobble out onto the stage, and to avoid embarrassing him, he would be in position before they opened the curtains.

Derek Prince happened to be on the same program with him that day. Derek has a ministry of holding people's feet, and having those whose legs are not the same length grow out to be equal. Through this approach, he has often seen God take care of all the other illnesses a person may have in addition.

The crippled minister introduced the issue on everyone's mind, by saying, "Many of you are probably wondering why I don't have Derek hold my feet." He continued, "I don't need anyone to hold my feet, because I was healed 2000 years ago; *by His stripes I was healed.* It's an accomplished fact, and I'm just waiting for the manifestation."

But you see the fallacy of that doctrine was that the crippled minister had God in a "faith box." In essence, he was not permitting God to do *His* work, *His* way. He was saying that "God will not do anything beyond my faith of what He can do," and that "God will not work in any way outside of my own, predetermined ways." He was not allowing God to be God. He was not allowing God to have one of *His* agents pray for him. I believe that God had arranged for him to be on the same platform with Derek, a man whom God had mightily anointed with a healing ministry, who even "specialized" in short legs.

Regrettably, he had God in such a faith box that it prevented him from receiving the healing ministry that may have been available to him that day. It's important to be flexible, to allow God to be God, and to allow God to be sovereign.

## Other Ways of Putting God in a Box

Anyone who limits God by saying, "I'll only be prayed for in my church, in my Methodist church, or my Presbyterian church, or Baptist Church;" or by a particular person, or who says "I can only be prayed for with the laying on of hands," or "I'll accept the anointing with oil, but none of that deliverance stuff," is also putting God in a box.

The girl with the frozen shoulder would still have a frozen shoulder, if she had said, "I don't believe in demons, I couldn't have a demon, don't pray against it as if it's a demon." The blind man in Scripture would still be blind, had he refused to allow Jesus to apply mud and spit to his eyes.

## "Are You in an Environment of Faith?"
## (The Company You Keep)

Attitudes, such as unbelief, doubt, and others, definitely

affect us, and can erode our faith. By contrast, if we are surrounded by believers who are in agreement about healing, we can have our faith increased regarding our healing or for the healing of others.

For example, to be in a Kathryn Kuhlman meeting was to be in an almost tangible atmosphere of faith and expectancy for God to move. The place was charged with faith, almost like with electricity, and provided an atmosphere in which healing thrived.

Conversely, one cannot feed continually on unbelief and at the same time maintain a healthy faith. For example, the person who experiences a miraculous healing and then decides to remain in a "dead to faith," anti- healing atmosphere, a church for instance that believes healing isn't for today, may lose that faith for healing or fall prey to some other malady. The belief and teaching of a church or Bible study group impacts the faith of its members. Without a belief in healing, people will begin to wonder why they aren't growing spiritually, or in faith; why they haven't made progress in their spiritual walk, and may complain to God that they have lost a sense of His power.

Paul refused to sit under what he knew to be false teaching for *even one hour*. Can we say the same?

## Cause and Effect

We in this modern age have been trained to think in terms of "cause and effect." When we see an effect, or a result, we expect to be able to find the cause. In the secular world this approach is laudable, however in the area of theology it readily leads man astray, usually causing him to blame God for the work of Satan. We know that we (and others) do sin, and assume that the problems we experience must result from the sin. This is not a new problem, the Pharisees saw the results that Jesus obtained in healing through deliverance, and credited the source of his power to Beelzebub, or Satan. (Mat. 2:24)

A major tenet of Jewish thought from earliest time has been that affliction was a sign of God's displeasure – that He punishes man with affliction and tragedy (consider the arguments of Job's friends). Jesus definitely refutes this hard-hearted mind-set with His teaching and examples of the Tower of Siloam (Luk. 13:4 – the eighteen were not the greatest sinners) and the man born blind (Jn. 9:2 – neither this man nor his parents sinned).

In our day a train crashes: 128 people are killed, two survive. The two survivors become committed Christians. A well-intentioned Christian attempting to make sense of it, judging from the good result, explains, "God caused that train wreck to save those two souls." RIDICULOUS! Did Jesus have to kill 64 people to save you?

The Scriptural truth of the matter is found in Romans. God can, and does, bring good out of the worst tragedies that can happen. That does not mean that in order to bring about the good, that He first had to cause the evil. Satan and disobedience to God cause the tragedies in the world. God gave man the wonderful gift of free will, which is only brings blessings, when used in obedience to God's will.

*And we know that **all things work together for good** to them that love God, to them who are the called according to his purpose.* Rom 8:28

## The Sovereignty of God

Another barrier to faith in healing is a misunderstanding of the word "sovereign." Satan has used the doctrine of "the sovereignty of God" as a powerful weapon to keep Christians in the dark about the true nature and love of God, and to cause fear, confusion and doubt about the will of

God. This doctrine implies that God may act erratically: He usually does good, but can do evil, if He wishes to accomplish good in the long run, such as the train wreck example given earlier.

Because this doctrine is so widespread and so damaging to faith, let's review Webster's definition of the word "sovereign."

> **1**.Chief or highest; supreme. **2**. Supreme in power; superior in position to all others; specif., princely; royal. **3**. Independent of and unlimited by, any other; possessing, or entitled to, original and independent authority or jurisdiction. **Syn.** Dominant," which lists: **"sovereign**, to that in comparison with every other thing of its kind is subordinate, inferior, or of lower value."

The above qualities all would aptly and validly apply to the Godhead. God is *sovereign,* a beneficent ruler, and no one can cause Him to alter His nature of total goodness:

> *And Jesus said unto him, Why callest thou me good? there is none **good** but one, **that is, God**.*
>
> Mark 10:18

The above passage does not imply that Jesus is not good, but that He is God! Nothing in the definition of sovereign implies that the good, sovereign, ruler, will be capricious, arbitrary, irrational, cruel, heartless, merciless, a torturer or murderer (those attributes do accurately describe the activities of His chief enemy). Our Heavenly Father expects His children to manifest the *fruit of His Spirit.* We need to remind ourselves that God is compassionate and the author and designer of such fruit, and that He *is "longsuffering to us, not willing that any should perish."* God is love (1 Jn. 4:8). Love does its neighbor no ill. (Rom. 13:10)

God is good; totally good, there is no perverseness in

Him:

*...God is light, and in him is **no darkness** at all.*
1 John 1:5

*Every **good** gift and every **perfect** gift is from above,
and cometh down from the Father of lights, with whom
is **no variableness** ["changing," "fickleness"] neither
shadow of turning.*
James 1:17

God doesn't kill a child for some "higher purpose." A child gets up in the night, climbs out an open widow, and crawls out into the street, where it is hit and killed by a drunk driver. If you must blame someone, blame the parent who left the window open, blame the man for getting drunk, blame the bartender who sold him the liquor, blame the parking lot attendant who gave him his keys...blame anyone you wish, (correctly blame Satan), but *do not say that it was the will of God to kill the child!!!*

God's will and Word oppose all sins of excess, especially drunkenness.

### Are You in an Environment of Death?

John was brought to our meetings and began to believe for his healing from cancer, but then his wife decided that he should be put into a facility that would prepare him for death and free up her time. This meant that he would be surrounded by those who were ministering death, rather than life, to him – he was in an environment of death and exposed to the constant, fervent, expectancy of death. Naturally, this eroded whatever faith he might have had for his healing.

### Don't Limit Your Sight

In this modern, secular world we have been taught to think in terms of science and its view of what can been seen, felt, touched, or measured. But Jesus instituted a "walking by faith rather than by sight," that is the opposite for the spiritual man. Consider His instructions to Martha, prior to raising Lazarus from the dead; *"believe* [and then] *you shall see."*

*Jesus saith unto her, Said I not unto thee, that, if thou wouldest believe, thou shouldest see the glory of God?*
John 11:40

Likewise, we are told that faith and prayer are asking that the unseen become reality, and that even the impossible happen. Praise God that we have a Savior who is in the business of the impossible!

*Jesus said unto him, If thou canst believe, all things are possible to him that believeth.* Mark 9:23

## Do You Have A Double-Minded Block?

*But let him ask in faith, **nothing wavering**. For he that wavereth is like a wave of the sea driven with the wind and tossed. For let not that man think that he shall receive any thing of the Lord. A double minded man is unstable in all his ways.* James 1:6-8

Clearly, there is an effective block posed by unbelief, and here we see the Scriptural proof that a man who permits himself to be overcome by unbelief, or doubt, may lose his chance to receive.

I was much like the man described by James in 1970, when I was down with cancer. "Lord, please heal me of cancer, if you want to heal me, but if you don't want to heal me, I'll praise you with my dying breath." Or, "Lord, I sure would like you to heal me, but if you have a higher purpose

143

in me dying, I'll accept it, and I'll praise you with my dying breath."

I was that double minded man, unstable in all my ways! I could not ask wholeheartedly to be healed for many reasons, because I was not convinced that He wills to heal all, and that He hadn't given the cancer to me in the first place.

### Believing, or Faith, is a Powerful Force

There is tremendous power in what we believe. This is why sometimes people get healed under false religions: their belief is that there is power present there to heal them, and this may help bring it into being. I personally doubt that such healings last or that they come at no cost (see occult healing exchange in Chapter Three.) Faith can be real in the kingdom of God and in the satanic kingdom of the counterfeit.

### What You Believe Can Heal, or Kill You

There was a case several years ago, in one of the major St. Louis hospitals, of man who was diagnosed with terminal cancer. He received prayer through a group of men, who visited him in the hospital to pray for him, and subsequent medical tests confirmed that he no longer had any trace of cancer! However, the man remained unconvinced. He believed that he still had cancer and that the doctors weren't telling him the truth. He sought second opinions, but they also confirmed his healing. The man died several months later, but the autopsy showed no cancer in his body. It appears that his *belief that he was dying* sufficed to kill him, in some way.

### Believing in *Faith* Healing.

I do not place my faith in "faith healers." The only proper place for faith, and source for faith, is in Jesus Christ who is the Healer. We look to the Giver and not the gift.

## Have You Placed Your Faith for Healing in Your Own Faith, or Even Magic?

People can have prideful, truth-blocking faith in their own faith. We've often had people come for healing who say, "I've got all the faith in the world," or say, "God should heal me, because I have faith. I have great faith!" And then they quote a Scripture.

But when I inquire, "What does that Scripture mean?"

They usually respond, "Well, I don't know, but somebody told me that if I repeated that verse every day, God would heal me."

This person is believing in magic; believing in a superstitious repetition like knocking on wood, or an "open sesame" magical incantation. Their trust is not in Jesus, nor in believing the promises in the Word of God, or even in that passage of Scripture. Their trust is, instead, in merely mechanically repeating phrases or words, because they hope that their incantation is going to bring about a healing.

*Jesus* **is the central, crucial issue in faith, and in healing.**

## Are You Trusting in Someone Else's Faith?

Another similar problem is relying on the faith of someone else. Sometimes people come for prayer saying, "Well, I believe that *you* can heal me."

Fortunately most don't believe that, but for those who do, they are putting their trust in someone, or something *other than Jesus*. And the basis for approaching Jesus for healing *you* of cancer is not the fact that He healed me of cancer, nor the fact that I say that He's a healer, but the fact that Jesus, Himself, says that He is a healer. The only correct basis on which to rightfully approach Jesus as the Healer is to humbly trust in His goodness, His pattern of healing in the Scripture, and God's promises for Healing.

Faith must be in Jesus, in the Rock, and in His promises.

As an example of the problem of looking to someone else's faith, I'll never forget one rather unpleasant experience I had years ago. One afternoon a woman called for an appointment for prayer. Her conversation began,

"Well my other 'healer' has died, and I've been referred to you."

She obviously had faith in some person, whom I suspect from the rest of the conversation probably used Tarot cards; it definitely was not a normal, Christian type of healing that she'd been involved with.

The proof of my suspicions came when she followed up by saying, "I'm Jewish, and I don't want you to use the Name of Jesus when you pray for me."

Well, needless to say I told her that for me to talk to her about healing, without talking about Jesus, would be black magic, and I would have nothing to do with it, and she had come to the wrong person.

Well that wasn't what she wanted to hear, and she proceeded to blast me in her syrupy sweet style. Her attitude, nonetheless, was an affront to me, and an affront to my God, to expect Him to heal her on *her terms*.

All I could say was "Ma'am, you've called the wrong person."

Thus, as we have seen, faith is a gift, given by God, and therefore it ill behooves any of us to criticize anyone else for a lack of faith.

* * *

If you have seen blocks in this chapter that you feel relate to you, you might start your prayer:

146

*Lord Jesus, I thank you for the gift of the faith which I now possess, and I ask You to forgive me, if I have limited Your working by inadequate faith. Forgive me also for unbelief, and for boxing you either in or out. Strengthen me now in my inner man and quicken to me the faith that I need.*

\* \* \*

"I can feel my faith for healing growing, what else do I need? I'm ready to do whatever I need to do, so that God may receive glory out of my healing."

For a more complete answer to the "You don't have enough faith" issue, see the author's book, *Three Kinds of Faith for Healing.* Available from Impact Christian Books.

# Chapter 10

# "How Desperate Are You?"

### "Are You Desperate Enough?"

The individuals who were healed in the Gospels were driven by holy desperation out into the wilderness to find an itinerant preacher/teacher named Jesus, whom they had heard was healing all who came to Him. The multitudes were so desperate that they sought Jesus in the **wilderness** (Mat. 13;30-33), in the **desert** (Mk.1:45, Lk. 9:10-11), in the **Temple** (Mat. 21:14), in the **cities** and **villages** (Mk. 6:56), in the **plain** (Mk. 6:17), and at the **seashore** (Mk. 3:7). Jesus healed them all, and at all those locations.

Similarly, today, one must be desperate enough to put forth an effort to reach Jesus, or His ministerial agents, for healing.

### "Have You Sought God Wholeheartedly?"

In addition to putting forth an effort, one must seek God with one's whole heart. God promises success if we do so:

*And ye shall seek me, and find me, when ye shall search for me with **all your heart**.*　　　Jer. 29:13

### "Are You Willing to Overcome Opposition?"

I have often joked that I would like to have a dime for every person who has had a flat tire, dead battery, or worse, on their way to come for prayer ministry. It is amazing how much *opposition* Satan puts forth in an attempt to prevent individuals from receiving the help they need. Numerous individuals have reported getting sick, having accidents etc., when they attempted to seek deliverance or healing.

This really shouldn't surprise us. We find many examples of opposition encountered by those seeking healing for themselves or family members in the Scriptures: the men carrying the man with palsy to see Jesus couldn't get through the crowd and so had to open up the roof of the house and to lower him through the roof; the woman with the flow of blood was barely able to reach the hem of Jesus' garment because of the pressing crowd. Yet, they and others did *persevere* in their attempts, and their needs were met.

## Expect Opposition from the World

The world cannot grasp the things of the kingdom of God, and certainly rejects healing or any other demonstration of the power of God which might tend to convict them of their own powerlessness. Jesus often encountered this kind of opposition, as He did (1) after delivering the Gadarene demoniac, when the townspeople begged Him to leave their country, and (2) at the house of Jairus, when He arrived to raise his daughter from the dead. The world's reaction was expressed in that room by the mourners, who ridiculed Him for thinking He could help. *And they laughed him to scorn.*

Remember the multitudes rebuked the blind men for trying to get Jesus' attention (Mat. 20:31). Even His own disciples tried to discourage the Syrophoenecian woman, and asked Jesus to send her away (Mat. 13:23).

## Opposition from Family, Friends

If you are trying to trust in God, and are seeking a healing, you can expect opposition not only from the world, but also from family, friends, and often even from the clergy. As sad as this is, the Devil comes at us from any available angle.

## Opposition from the Religious World

The religious leaders of Jesus' day said He was in league with the Devil and worked his miracles by Satan's power. The religious rulers so opposed His healing ministry, that they excommunicated the blind man whose sight was restored (John 9:34)! Is there much difference today?

Today the religious, scholarly elite say the same kind of things, or they may be more subtle in their attack. When my wife, Sue, and I first considered going to a Kathryn Kuhlman meeting, she asked the advice of a family friend. He was a minister, so she wanted to know what he thought of Kathryn Kuhlman. And his response was, "Oh she's a phony, she's a fake. Going won't do you any good."

That is the world's view. It's also, tragically, the view of much of the church leadership. Even though our family friend was clergy, he still had a world's eye view of the things of the kingdom, and stood in the way of the power of God. Unfortunately, many of the "ungifted" in the church structure have that same world's eye view of the Holy Spirit's gifts and the overall gifted kingdom.

The natural world *cannot see* the kingdom of God (Jn. 3:3), nor can they grasp the reality of God's healing power at work today. It is also a threat to some religious leaders because, if God is working in this way, then they are missing God. It is also a sign to them of their own insignificance, in part, when compared to the power and might of the Holy Spirit.

Today far too many in the clergy have largely abdicated their role of providing healing for the sheep under their care to the doctors, and have joined the unsaved in directing believers to the world of the "professionals."

\* \* \*

If you have seen blocks in this chapter that you feel relate to you, you might start your prayer:

*Lord, I do want to seek You with my whole heart and I determine to resist all opposition.*

\* \* \*

"But *should I* seek medical help?"

# Chapter 11

# "What About Doctors and Medicine?"

### "Should I Seek Medical Help?"

I praise God for good doctors and nurses, who are able to help alleviate suffering. There is nothing wrong with going to a doctor, or in seeking medical aid for your condition. Like many of us, you may need some help, until your faith developes to a point that you no longer need outside assistance.

Remember also, someone needs to care for those who do not have faith. The ideal goal, however, should definitely be to have your own faith grow, develop, and mature to the point that you are able to walk by faith. As soon as you are able to do so, it is advisable to trust Jesus exclusively for your health: He is less expensive; He never makes mistakes; there are no after-effects or side-effects; and even if you do not reach Him in time for your healing, He will still take care of you.

The question comes to mind, how do the sick Christians in the poorest countries of the world which do not have access to modern medical assistance, such as many African nations, survive?

The decision to rely only on Jesus, however, cannot be made for you by anyone else, nor should it be made by yourself alone. This issue can only be decided for you by Jesus.

Are you trusting solely in Jesus? I have met several people over the years whose testimony was, "I have trusted

Jesus exclusively for my health and haven't taken any medicine or seen a doctor in over twenty years." I must confess I am not personally operating at that level, but it is challenging and faith-building to know that there are those who are.

### "Do You Have A Jesus-*Plus* Something Block?"

Anytime you get into Jesus plus something, you're no longer seeking God 100 percent, with your whole heart. If I'm putting my trust in horses or chariots, or in peach pits, or in eating black mushrooms in France at midnight, my trust is not completely in Him. We may laugh at the thought of trusting in mushrooms, but I received a call late one night from a man who told me he had a "national traveling healing ministry" and his wife had developed cancer. He called to tell me, surprisingly enough, that he was taking her to France to have "black mushrooms picked at midnight, so she could eat them." He had heard that these particular mushrooms were a miracle cure, and wanted to know what I thought of the idea.

I replied bluntly, but truthfully, "I think that sounds like the weirdest thing I've ever heard. It sounds occult."

He didn't want to hear that, because his faith was in the black mushrooms, and he seriously believed, somehow, they were going to heal his wife. I never heard from him again, so I assume the trip wasn't successful.

Anytime we're going to put our trust in any other source, in Jesus-*plus* something else: black mushrooms, powdered milk, nutrition, protein, Jesus-*plus* vitamins, Jesus-*plus* health foods, or Jesus-*plus* fortune-tellers or rabbit's feet, we really are not trusting in Jesus! I once was denounced by a man who ran a health food store, because I wasn't recommending health food supplements when I taught on healing. Incidentally, if you look at the books displayed in the average health food store, you will find that most of the titles are fear-based, if not partially or overtly occult.

It's been said 'we should do what we can do (eat right, get adequate rest and the like), and then trust Jesus to do what we cannot. Note that I am not saying that taking vitamins is evil (I take some myself). But just look at the suggested reading at the health food store, and see if you don't see a lot of marginally or overtly occult material, New Age writing, and authors like the Maharajah of this, and the Guru of that.

### "Are You Expecting Magic, or Showmanship?"

Many people are expecting magic, or some kind of a spectacular show – something other than simple prayer and simply going to the Word of God. That's why the charlatans can succeed, and lure people in. They put on a big show, and tend to offer something more than just the simple, unadulterated Word of God.

An old Pentecostal pastor who attended our meetings regularly until he passed away, said something that was interesting: "I've tried to tell some of our preachers that they can just stand up and proclaim the Word like you do, but they don't believe it. They feel that they've got to have all the pomp, and put on a good show. They don't believe that the Word of God alone will do it."

Sometimes, even preachers aren't willing to simply place their trust in the Word, which they are proclaiming.

### "But I have Been Prayed For at My Own Church."

Don't limit yourself. Your church may definitely be one of the best in your area, but it may not have an anointing for healing. Do not deny yourself the opportunity to seek healing elsewhere. The true Church, after all, is much larger than your congregation, it's worldwide! Consider the ministry of Kathryn Kuhlman and many of those who have had great healing crusades. Don't you think most of the people, who attended and were healed, had been prayed for before? You bet they had.

If you read any of Kathryn Kuhlman's books, which record the great miracles that occurred in her services, you will be struck by the fact that in almost every case the person made *a journey* to find their healing. Often that journey required a "stepping out in faith" against great odds.

### "But I Was Diagnosed by a Christian Doctor."

One of the most interesting healings of deafness we encountered was that of a couple who came to visit our meetings because they had heard that deaf ears were being opened. As mentioned before, in a period of about three months we witnessed about 120 deaf ears healed by Jesus!

The couple had traveled from a Southern state, and the woman came up for prayer first. She said, "I'm 85% deaf in one ear and nearly 100% deaf in the other. My husband is only 50% deaf in one ear and 75% deaf in the other, but we *will both be totally deaf within a year."*

"How on earth could you possibly know that?" I asked incredulously.

"Because we are partners with the ministry of a Christian hospital. We went for a free annual check up and the *Christian doctor* there told us so."

Sensing we were on to something, I asked "Did you have trouble hearing before you went? Is that why you had your hearing tested?

"Oh, no, it was a routine physical. We had no hearing trouble before that time last year. We could hear perfectly."

I suggested, as gently as I could, "I think you picked up a spirit of deafness from that diagnosis. If you had been given that prediction of deafness by a fortune-teller, you would instantly renounce it, right? However, you naturally believed the Christian doctor when he said that you were going deaf. To put it in the kindest light, let's assume that his equipment was off that day and you received a misdiagnosis. I'm going to pray against a spirit of deafness in both of you."

I then prayed and commanded the spirit of deafness to come out of the ears of both of them, and we also renounced the acceptance which allowed it to so easily enter. After praying for their healing, we tested the hearing of each of them by having them face away from me. I walked progressively further away behind them, until I was standing twenty-five feet away from them and whispering softly. Each was able to repeat every word that I whispered! Our testing methods were admittedly unsophisticated, but the fact of their healing was evident to all. They realized it as well and rejoiced!

### "God Can't (Or Won't) Heal Me<br>Because I've Sought Medical Help," or<br>"Because I've Taken Medication, etc."

I can offer two answers for this objection: one from Scripture; one from experience. First consider the case of the woman with the flow of blood, whom "Dr." Luke records as having, "spent all her living upon physicians, neither could be healed of any." Did her having desperately sought the assistance of the physicians make her ineligible for the healing touch of Jesus? It did not.

Next, it is obvious that if someone were to have an organ removed, God could not heal *that* organ. However, He could still recreate or give you a replacement. He did just that for a man who came to our meeting about twenty years ago! He said, "I want prayer, because I have a tumor behind my ear, and I have been diagnosed as being totally deaf in my left ear."

After prayer, he was able to hear clearly out of his left ear. About three months later, however, he did have the tumor surgically removed. And, about a month afterwards he again appeared at our meeting, this time with a paper in his hand stating, "This certifies that I am eligible for disability, because they had to remove all the hearing organs of my left ear, when they took the tumor. But, God healed me before and I believe He can restore my hearing, even now!"

Awed by his evident faith, we prayed for that brother, and God *restored the hearing in his ear, which had no eardrum!*

**God is limited only by our grasp of His capacity to heal! And His love knows no bounds.**

## Ministering to Those Wounded By Warped Doctrines

My wife and I would probably describe ourselves as Charismatic, in that we believe that all the gifts of the Spirit are for today. However, Sue and I have spent much of the last thirty-plus years ministering to those who have been devastated by bad teaching and warped doctrines – the confused, the spiritually hurt and wounded. These people were left feeling that they in some way failed God, or had been rejected by God when a doctrine, which they'd accepted, didn't work for them.

### "Why Has God Failed Us?"

One day a couple from a local fellowship came to my prayer room in tears, devastated and crushed. They said "We really need to talk to you." They then explained that they couldn't understand why God had failed to honor their faith.

They sat in my prayer room and told me the tragic story of how they had been in a church caught up in the "name-it-and-claim-it" doctrine. As a result of that teaching, they had repeatedly, publicly, confessed that their children were going to have their teeth straightened by the Lord, without needing braces before school started the following September. When September rolled around, and the teeth had not straightened, they were embarrassed, and frustrated. Their children were similarly embarrassed, because they also had been confessing publicly that their teeth were going to be straightened by the Lord.

"Then, when school started, we had to put the kids in braces, because their teeth weren't straightened. How did we fail God?"

"I don't believe you have failed God at all. He still loves you. Perhaps you boxed God into a time frame, that it had to be done by September 1st, and maybe that wasn't God's timing. You know the enemy always fights up to the very last moment. Many times we hear testimonies of 'eleventh hour' deliverances." There is always the issue of timing. (Discover more truth about "Timing" in Chapter 12.)

## Dangers of Name-It-And-Claim-It Theology

The name-it and claim-it doctrine was one that we encountered quite often in the early days. Did you ever stop to think that if the name-it and claim-it concept were valid, that Jesus and Peter could have gotten together after the Sermon on the Mount, and claimed the soul of every person who would be born on earth? They could have saved us all the troubles and torments of the last 20 centuries. But they did not and they could not, because it was not within the will of God to do it that way, even though God desires for all to come to saving faith.

Note well, however, that there is a valid place for the prayer of agreement; for two believers to be drawn together, to pray in agreement for a desired outcome. The scripture implies in the Greek "to be led together in harmony" or "in symphony" by the Holy Spirit who is the conductor of the orchestra, who leads two together in one accord, and one in agreement. Therefore, it is valid for them to pray for whatsoever they will, within the limitation of being within the will of God, as John teaches:

> And this is the confidence that we have in him, that, if we **ask any thing according to his will**, he heareth us: And if we know that he hear us, whatsoever we ask, we know that we have the petitions that we desired of him.                              1 John 5:14-15

## "Should I Take My Medicine?"

Another case we encountered was that of a man on the verge of tears, who came to see me saying he desperately needed an appointment. We went into my prayer room, and as soon as he sat down he began to cry, sobbing out, "I've failed God. Tell me what I've done wrong."

I asked, "What makes you think that you've failed God?"

He said, "Because I trusted Him for my healing, and I woke up in Barnes Hospital, where they told me I almost died."

Curious, I inquired, "How did that come about?"

He explained, "Well I'm a diabetic, and I went to see a minister, "John Jones," (whom I knew had unsuccessfully attempted ministry, and then gone to a Bible college to obtain certification that he was a "man of God," and a "faith" minister). He counseled me, and prayed for me to be healed. Then he told me, 'We've prayed once, and that's all there is to it. It is done, and you should never take any medicine again.'"

He continued, "The next thing I knew, I woke up in Barnes Hospital, having nearly died."

I said, "Well brother, the *second* mistake you've made is telling me this story. The *first* mistake was listening to him in the first place. The second mistake is sitting here telling *me*: you ought to be sitting in *his* chair telling *him*, before he kills someone!"

Now, there is a valid place for a 'quickening' (in Greek, *rhema*) from God, that leads you to do something, even to stop medication, *if He tells you to do so.* However, there are two sources of information and voices in the Spirit realm. And this is why it becomes important not to be in a rush, and to verify the source. The Lord usually speaks, and then *confirms His word to you, out of the mouths of two or three other witnesses.*

There was another case that occurred in our area a few years ago. A woman was in the shower, and heard an audible voice that said, "Flush your medicine down the toilet."

She couldn't believe what she was hearing. She turned the shower off; and looked around the corner very carefully, to see if there was someone in the bathroom with her. There wasn't, but again she heard the voice, and it said more firmly, "Flush your medicine down the toilet!"

So she went and got all her medicine and flushed it down the toilet, and was completely healed. But it *wasn't me* telling her to do that, it wasn't *you* telling her that, it was the voice of God, Himself, telling her to do that, and that's the difference. **I would be very skeptical of anyone who attempts to tell you to stop taking your medication.**

Many people seem to feel that they must quit taking their medication as a sign of their faith, or to prove to God

161

that they have the faith to be healed. God is powerful enough to make you well even while you are taking medication. He is capable of making you so well that, for example, if you were formerly diabetic, even *your doctor* will have to recognize that you no longer need insulin.

Most doctors acknowledge that although they aid in the process, they cannot heal. For example, for a doctor to give medicine to, or operate on, a dead man...will the patient improve? Obviously not. The force of life must be present, as James states:

> *For as the body without the spirit is dead, so faith without works is dead also.* James 2:26

To briefly recap: 1.) It's okay to seek good medical help when needed. 2.) It's equally important to remain open to hear from God concerning your steps to recovery; the best scenario would be to access a Spirit-filled group that hears from the Lord, adminsters the laying on of hands and is willing to encourage and pray with you. 3.) Be willing to hear from God, if He should speak to you to avoid certain procedures or medications – but that is strictly between you and the Lord. 4.) Finally, recognize that God can heal you even while you are seeking medical assistance.

* * *

If you have seen blocks in this chapter that you feel relate to you, you might start your prayer:

> *Lord, I thank you for those who are able to help me while I am hurting and awaiting your healing touch...*

* * *

"When will my healing arrive?"

# Chapter 12

# "Is It Time For My Healing?"

### "Do You Recognize the Difference
### Between a *Miracle* and a *Healing*?"

Another truth we must keep in mind is that a **healing** and a **miracle** are two different demonstrations of God's power; they are not the same. The two words are not synonymous. Satan has used our misunderstanding of these two words perhaps more than anything else to rob Christians of their blessing s of healings.

A "miracle" happens in the twinkling of an eye: blind eyes open, cripples walk, deaf ears open. An *instantaneous* healing is a "miracle" by scriptural definition.

On the other hand, my healing from cancer was a "healing," by scriptural definition, in that it took seven months instead of seven seconds. Nonetheless powerful, nonetheless effective, it still took time. *A healing takes time.*

The truth just stated is also borne out in the words of Jesus Himself. Jesus said, "Believers shall lay hands upon the sick and the sick *shall recover*" (Mk. 16:18). *Shall* implies future action; *to recover* implies something happening in the future. The promise applies equally to those "healed" immediately, and to those whose recovery requires some time!

It's extremely important that we recognize the distinction between the two, miracles and healings, in the event we have not received an instantaneous miracle. We

163

need to persevere and to hold on, waiting in faith for the fulfilling of the promise.

### Scriptural Evidence of Healings vs. Miracles

In addition to the words above from Jesus Himself, there are other confirmations of this truth in the Scripture. For example, Paul also apparently differentiates between healings and miracles in I Corinthians 12:9-10, when he mentions the two different gifts "of healings and "of working of miracles." In addition, perhaps, an example of a healing is to be seen in the case of the ten lepers whose healings occured on their way to see the priests (Lk. 17:14-15). Jesus moved so powerfully in the working of miracles that most frequently, those in need whom *He* touched received "miracles."

Often, He stretches our faith, and at the very last moment, when all seems lost, God's healing becomes evident in the physical. That is, it is important to again point out that there is generally a spiritual battle of some form going on in the heavenlies around someone who is sick. This is especially the case for those who face life-threatening sicknesses. Often, the greater the battle, the longer the battle is, and the greater the victory in the end.

However, the Scriptural key to understand the difference between a healing and miracle is in the *evidence seen*. Faith, to which we have access thanks to our relationship with Jesus Christ, is evidence of things *not seen*. Therefore, there is an underpinning assumption that our healing may be achieved in the spiritual realm in advance of the evidence of healing in the physical realm. That may not bring great comfort for those in pain, but I often wonder at what point, in my own battle with cancer, the victory was decided in heaven even while it took seven months to work its way out in the physical realm on earth. Bizarre to imagine from our human point of view, but things in the spiritual are often decided before they bear themselves out in the physical.

How do we know the outcome, then, in advance? The evidence that we are given to hold on to is twofold: 1.) the general promises in the Word regarding God's will to heal us, and 2.) the specific, personal promises that the Lord will speak directly to us, as confirmation that the battle is His and not ours, and that the battle has already been won! God still speaks to His children, and in a variety of manners. However, these promises often combine specific Biblical verses with words spoken at opportune moments by someone moving in the Holy Spirit. (In the most desperate of situations, the Lord will even use the title of a secular book, for instance, or the mouth of an unbeliever, to confirm His promises to you. We have seen it!)

This is what I meant when I spoke earlier of a *rhema*, or "quickening," of the Holy Spirit.  It also emphasizes how important it is to try to get into the company of people active in the gifts of the Holy Spirit.  Or at the least, people who are yielded to the Spirit's wisdom and knowledge.  This allows His specific words to you to be quickened, and to be delivered speedily!

Even if you are unable to find such people to minister the Lord's knowledge, pray that the Lord will use the people around you to confirm His specific promises. I have received confirmations from people who didn't have a clue that they were being used by the Spirit.

When we receive these confirmations, then our assurance is as good as gold, as solid as stone. Once the Lord has spoken, and we have received confirmation in some form, then we know, beyond any shadow of a doubt, that God has already worked out the details of our healing! The outcome is more of a reality than the four walls in the room around you! And then we can have the patience and perseverance to "be still and know."

## "Why Do Some Unbelievers Receive Miracles?"

Many believers find it difficult to understand why unbelievers often seem to receive miracles, while they have to struggle in faith to receive. This is another important aspect of the distinction between a miracle and a healing. God can only reasonably expect faith from believers.

God heals us, because of His great love for His creation, mankind. He wants us to love Him in return. One of the normal fruits of a healing, is a great love for God, who has so mericifully dealt with us. A healing normally draws one either into a relationship with God, or deeper into a relationship which already existed.

He cannot expect unbelievers to exercise faith, awaiting the arrival of their healing. Therefore, oftentimes *unbelievers* are blessed with miraculous healings, where the physical and the spiritual battles are resolved at once. Whereas *believers* often receive healings, where there is an apparent gap in timing of the resolution of the two.

This is not a hard, fast rule, but I have seen it enough to raise the suspicion that there may be a spiritual trend at work. If those without Jesus had not received a miracle, they perhaps would never have been healed, and most importantly, the hope of them receiving their salvation would be less likely. We see the link between healing as an effective tool of salvation in Jesus' own words:

> *"When you enter a town and are welcomed, eat what is set before you. Heal the sick who are there and tell them, 'The kingdom of God is near you.'"*
>
> Luke 10:8-9

Notice that Jesus put an order to His words of evangelism: first heal the sick, and then preach to them the news of the kingdom of God! Healings are often used by God to draw the unsaved, like a dinner bell, to a place where they can receive the Bread of Heaven. An excellent example of this principle is provided in Scripture.

> *Then Philip went down to the city of Samaria, and preached Christ unto them. And the people with one accord gave heed unto those things which Philip spake, hearing and seeing the miracles which he did. For unclean spirits, crying with loud voice, came out of many that were possessed with them: and many taken with palsies, and that were lame, were healed.*
>
> Acts 8:5-7

Because of His great love for man, the Lord sometimes moves on man's behalf and in spite of man. Oddly enough, there is a certain logic to that. God cannot expect an unbeliever to await in faith, or on the basis of faith in the promise of healing, as yet unfulfilled. But He can expect believers, who have faith or growing faith, to await the fulfillment of their promise.

### "Why Is My Healing Taking So Long? There May Be Good Reason

Something else we need to remember is that God often wants to work things into us, or out of us. And so He may turn the battle being waged through the healing process into an accomplishment of His purposes. Just remember this important truism: **a delay in the fulfillment of the physical battle is not a no**!

I think one of the reasons that it took seven months to heal me, from start to finish, was because there were a lot of things God wanted to work into me, and a lot of things He had to work out of me, prior to being healed. Additionally, there may have been a specific thing that I needed to learn, some Scripture that I need to discover, because I would need it desperately in another area or at a future point. In my own case, I praise God that I wasn't healed in seven seconds instead of seven months. It taught me the truth that healings take time. And I know that truth with assurance, even while the battle rages around me,

> *...we know that all things work together for good to them that love God*        Rom. 8:28

During that delay, I was led to travel 20,000 miles in search of healing from, and truth about, the Holy Spirit. And I was caused to delve deeply into the Word of God to find answers. I was being taught by the Spirit about healing, and healing for myself. I praise God that I wasn't healed in a Kathryn Kuhlman meeting. Had I been, if ever I were to be sick again, I would have gone back to her meetings for another healing. That is where my faith would have been. But because I wasn't healed in her meeting, I learned to seek God on my own, and was empowered to find the Healer on my own. This was to prove necessary, so that when I was sick and unable to go to her meetings (as since she has died), I could go directly to Him. Likewise, I was taught that the Lord does not use just one agent, in this case Miss Kuhlman, to minister healing, but he has raised many men and women yielded to His Spirit and His power.

### Failing to Allow for God's Timing
God's timing is always perfect, but His timing is often *not our timing*. We tend to be impatient. We want it now, immediately; and God often delivers at the eleventh hour.

### Not Awaiting the Promise's Fulfillment
Again, once you have received a promise from God that you can trust for your healing, then you must make your

stand in faith, awaiting the fulfillment of your promised healing. It takes no faith on my part to believe that you are going to give me an apple, once you have placed it in my hand. **Faith only comes into play when there is a delay between the promise and its fulfillment.** So, be patient and trust God to deliver! Don't give up too soon, before your miracle arrives. And sometimes, in the darker moments, it is necessary to get more prayer, and to ask for more confirmation, if you need encouragement.

### Roxanne's Picture of Timing

Roxanne Brant, a beautiful young woman, who had a healing ministry very similar to that of Kathryn Kuhlman, shared with me her understanding of the operation and the timing of God in healing. She gave the following visual illustration: *Healing* is like a picture to be hung on the wall. The nail upon which it is to be hung is *the will of God*. The string or wire by which the picture is supported is the *timing of God*.

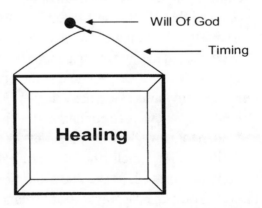

In some cases, the time has not yet been fulfilled for a healing to be manifested. God does things perfectly: in the perfect, fullness of time. As an example, consider my friend, the surgeon.

169

### "Have I Failed God?"

A friend of mine was a well-respected doctor who, along with his wife, had received the Baptism in the Spirit in our prayer room years before. He stopped in to see me one afternoon, looking very down, "I have to talk to you, if you have some time. I really feel as if somehow I failed God, or maybe God failed me."

Once he was settled comfortably in my prayer room, I asked, "What's the problem?"

"I have to confess I feel a little embarrassed coming to you with this problem, because I know how much success you have had with healing bad backs in your ministry. I should have come to you earlier for prayer. I guess, I didn't even think of it at the time, but...I know you'll forgive me."

"However, here's what happened. About six months ago, I began experiencing numbness in my wrists and hands. As a surgeon *I have to have* full use of my hands. I prayed about it, and had prayer at my church, but when my hands didn't improve I went to see a specialist, who said I had a pinched nerve in my back, which would require surgery. I told the Lord that if it wasn't better by October, I would have to have the recommended surgery. The condition didn't improve, and I had the surgery, but I have been under terrible condemnation ever since." Almost at the point of tears, he continued, "Why didn't God heal me?"

"Well, we know that condemnation is not from the Lord." I then told my friend the surgeon, "Let's just assume, for the sake of an argument, that your prayer was heard, the moment it was prayed, as we know the Scripture tells us that it was. You prayed a prayer in accordance with the will of God to be healed. As in the case of Daniel (Dan. 10), your prayer was heard, the wheels in heaven were set in motion, the answer was dispatched. Let's also assume that God, in His loving compassion decided, 'I'm going to give

170

Dr. _____ a Christmas present, and on December 25th I'm going to heal him completely, the pinched nerve in his back along with restoration for his hands.'"

"I don't know that I have the complete answer for you, but in a number of cases I have seen people pray for something and then put God under a deadline, or time limit. You've asked me what you *did wrong*. I don't believe you did anything wrong, with the possible exception of not giving God enough time to complete the work in His own sovereign way, and in His own sovereign timing. I don't know if that's the full answer, but it's made sense to me in a number of similar cases."

Suddenly beaming, the doctor turned to me and said with a hug, "Thanks, Bill, that's the answer for me! That's exactly what I needed to hear! I'm rejoicing that I didn't fail God, and that God didn't fail me. I just didn't allow enough time." And he left refreshed with a tangible sense of the Lord's love. My friend's story about his back reminded me of the healings of two classic "bad back" cases.

## A Young Nun's Back Healed!

There was a young Nun who came to a healing service I was asked to conduct for a prayer group at a hospital in St. Louis. The Nun came forward for prayer, saying "I have five fused vertebrae in my spine as the result of an auto accident. And," her eyes began filling with tears, "I haven't been able to bend over and pick up my prayer book, or even to kneel in church for years."

After receiving prayer, I told her to try kneeling, which she did without pain, and then proceeded to bend forward to touch her toes several times!

Her healing resulted in great joy and praise to God, not only from the young Nun, but also from the onlookers, as did so many of the healing accounts in the Scripture.

# Tom's Crushed Disc Healed

Tom is my other favorite back story. When he came to see me, due to a strong, satanically inspired delay, he had to wait nearly an hour before I was able to pray with him. Tom introduced his problem saying, "I need to have my back healed, because I'm having terrible back pain. And I am going to have back surgery next Tuesday for a crushed disc. But I have to confess, I've been fearing coming to see you more than I have the doctor, or the surgery."

Surprised, I asked, "Why?"

"Because, I know that I need more than just a healing. Although I've gone to church all my life, I know I don't know Jesus the way all the rest of you people do, and like my wife does."

To make a long story short, Tom then agreed to receive Jesus as His Lord and Savior and the Baptism with the Holy Spirit. Then we prayed for his back. After praying, I told him, "Now, get up out of that chair, and without hurting yourself, try and find the pain in your back."

Still rather dazed from all the blessings he'd just received, Tom gingerly moved upward, gently twisting his torso. Then he announced, "We'll, there's no pain at all. I'm not going out and lift a sack of cement, but I have no pain!"

As if the Lord hadn't already been good enough to us, I received a further blessing. Tom was healed on a Saturday. The following Monday I had to do a television interview in Indiana. On the way back just south of Chicago, I got trapped in a snowstorm and had to stop at a motel to spend the night. I called my wife Monday evening to tell her I wouldn't be able to make it home. When she answered, I could tell from her tone that she had some exciting news. "Tom's wife called to tell me that he went to the hospital today for a pre-op appointment, and when they X-rayed his spine in order to mark his back with betadyne for the operation, they could not find any *trace* of a degenerated disc.  Tom said the doctor was angry and shouted at him to go home – because *he no longer needed the surgery!*"

Often God does choose to heal at the last possible moment.  Perhaps His reason for doing so is to stretch our faith, to test our faith, or it may be due to satanic opposition, but notice that *He does deliver.*  And as we have so often stated: "**a delay is not a no!**"

* * *

If you have seen blocks in this chapter that you feel relate to you, you might start your prayer:

*Lord, I thank You for showing me the difference between miracles and healings, and for showing me that Your timing in always perfect.  I am blessed to know that even though my healing hasn't yet arrived, it is on the way.*

* * *

As we have seen, many are adversely affected by their erroneous beliefs.

# Chapter 13

# "Is Bad Theology Killing You?"

Not only have we allowed our theology to be shaped by the world (as in the aforementioned, mislabeled "acts of God"), but we have also received a lot of bad teaching from our religious institutions. Tragically some denominations have taught or implied that God is wrathful and vengeful. They have presented a God who is "just waiting" for you to make a mistake, so that He can have the pleasure of punishing you: to strike you with a lightening bolt, or to inflict tragedy upon your life.

Likewise, they teach that God somehow has a part to play in the evil that plagues the earth. Would our God dirty His hands with Satanic inspired evil? They teach that while God does not will for bad things to happen, He permits them to happen; they are part of His "permissive will." And "with His permission" implies that He has passively participated in the act of ultimate evil, such as the case of a child killing or death of an infant as mentioned before. With this incredibly erroneous logic, they tarnish the reputation of a gracious and compassionate God with the works of Satan.

This obviously is a lie. And it comes from the author of lies, Satan. It is disproved by the numerous promises of the Lord's love, promises of His compassion and mercy and faithfulness. For instance,

*God is light, and in him is **no darkness** at all.*

1 John 1:5

*For this purpose the Son of God was manifested, that*
*he might **destroy** the works of the devil.*

1 John 3:8

An entire generation of religious leaders has been taught to tacitly attach blame to God for the evil that occurs in our lives, rather than placing the blame squarely on Satan, the "murderer from the beginning." This distorted indoctrination is also part of Satan's plan.

Satan will do anything he can in an attempt to discourage people from receiving the power of God in their lives. He will frighten people away from accepting Jesus as Savior, with lies like "God will send you to Africa," or "you will have to cut all ties to normal society." Likewise, he will do all in his power to prevent people from discovering that Jesus still heals today. Among the tools in his bag of tricks are rumor, innuendo, bad teaching, tradition, and fears of various kinds. In this section we will attempt to diffuse and debunk a number of his commonly used weapons and snares.

## Bad Theology Kills

Bad theology can kill! Bad theology can destroy us spiritually, because in its most dangerous form it says, "You don't need Jesus as Savior." This proves that bad theology can deny us salvation and eternal life, and that it can kill us spiritually.

In the same sense, bad theology can also kill us physically, because it says, **"Jesus no longer heals"**; or **"Healing is not for today."** Thus, it can deny us healing for our bodies, and destroy us physically.

A little over thirty years ago, I was one of those dying as a result of bad theology. I had been taught and believed that Jesus no longer healed the way He once did; that the miracles of the early church were a thing of the past, and that healing was not for today. As a result of that bad thinking, I was dying as a terminal cancer patient. Praise be to God, I learned the truth, rejected the lies, and was healed.

### "Why Should God Heal Me?"

One question I often use with people who need prayer is, "Why should God heal you?"

That helps determine a person's theology. It uncovers whether someone is coming in humility, or in pride or in ignorance of God. And it provides a clue as to whether he or she really knows Jesus.

The answer we often get is, "Sure, I'm good, I always try to do good." This shows that the person is relying upon his own righteousness, and lacks an understanding of the righteousness that is available through Jesus. Such individuals usually follow up by saying, "Well I've *never killed* anyone." We think we're good, because we've never killed anyone.

Often people may respond with overt pride, saying, "Well I deserve it as much as anyone else. He healed so-and-so, and I deserve it as much as he does."

Sometimes they are so blatant as to state their credentials: "I'm important, I'm a minister, I'm a business executive, I'm rich and successful." And such comments may be made by friends who have brought the candidate, saying of him, "He deserves it, he's a good person."

They may very well be correct: he or she may be a good person, but that doesn't provide the proper basis on which to approach Jesus. It is never an issue of our goodness. Rather it is the goodness of God that is going to produce the healing. He is the Giver of life and health.

It may help to think in terms of salvation. Salvation is not received on the basis of *our* goodness, but on the basis of *His* goodness. It's not of works lest any man boast (Eph. 2:8-9), but it is instead a matter of faith in His grace.

177

## The Case of A Skeptical Nun

I recall a nun who came to our prayer room, and received both a healing and the baptism with the Spirit. She commented afterwards, "Boy, this sure beats all those textbooks."

You see all those textbooks told her it wasn't necessary to be baptized with the Spirit, nor to speak in tongues, and that healing wasn't for today. And in light of hard facts and personal experience, those arguments all went out the window when she had a confrontation with the living Christ, who baptized her with the Spirit and healed her physically.

## "Why Can't God Heal Me in My Own Bedroom?"

Candidates for healing will often ask questions like, "Why hasn't God already healed me?" "Why do I have to come to a meeting and ask for prayer?" "Why didn't He do it at home in my bedroom [in private]?"

I usually answer, "If He had, you wouldn't be here. Perhaps God didn't do things that way, because He wanted you to humble yourself, wanted to let you to see the necessity of the ministry of His body, and the power and truth of this ministry for yourself. Perhaps, He wanted to have an opportunity to answer some of your questions, and to draw out of you any bad theology that might be standing in your way. Also, if you were healed in private, who would know? How could you prove it? By receiving your healing in a public setting, such as at a prayer meeting or healing service, God can not only give you a healing, but also a testimony as a bonus. Perhaps He can even use your own healing experience to begin equipping you for an area of ministry of your own!"

There is praying and there is praying. When I was dying of cancer thirty years ago, before I began my journey in search of healing, I and others in my family were praying

for my healing; praying hard, but not praying in faith –
praying without any grasp of God's will to heal; just praying as a typical Presbyterian, Baptist or Methodist might –
praying in hope and desperation.

There is a great difference in just praying at home and
hoping to be healed, and actively going in search of healing by stepping out "on the water" in faith, seeking to contact His healing power. Both the action of stepping out in
faith and the healing power present are excellent reasons
for attending a healing service. Be encouraged that,

> *The effectual fervent prayer of a righteous man*
> *availeth much.*                                    James 5:16

### "Are You Being Blocked by Traditions of Man?"

I was immediately confronted by the traditions of my
church when I began thinking about healing, and their limited thinking. My ministers were not familiar with healing
and therefore feared it. Healing is a threat to those who
have not embraced it.

You have probably heard the old saying, "The last seven
words of the church are, *We've never done that in our
church.*"

Do not let your friends, fellow church members or even
your own family dictate truth to you – they may, unknowingly, be killing you.

### "All Faith-healers Are Charlatans
### And Are Only in it for the Money."

It is true that charlatans and abuses do exist, but that
should not prevent you from seeking healing, any more
than the fact that there are counterfeiters should cause you
to throw away all your money! Remember, you're trusting
the words of Jesus Himself.

Would we consider that Jesus was a charlatan when

He healed the multitudes?  Or that His disciples in Acts were charlatans when they continued this healing ministry?  Clearly there is a validity to the power of God, despite the obvious abuses sometimes seen in the world today.

## Are You Harboring
## Anger, Bitterness, or Wrath?

We give the enemy a legal right to attack, or to gain a stronghold in our lives, when we harbor anger, unforgiveness, or bitterness. We expose ourselves to the agents of Satan, rather than to God, by such action. We need to walk in daily forgiveness and to make the decision not to go to bed angry.

> *Be ye angry, and sin not: let not the sun go down upon your wrath: Neither **give place** to the devil.*
> Eph. 4:26-27

This is the kind of theology that should be preached to those who are sick. When we forgive, we release blessing onto others, not based on what they have done, but based on the fact that Jesus commanded us to do so. We forgive because He first forgave us. Unforgiveness plays an enormous role in blocking healing and answers to prayer, and fueling the enemy's attack.

## Trusting in The Arm of the Flesh

We are warned not to look to man to have our needs met, but to look only to the Lord.

> *Put not your trust in princes, nor in the son of man, in whom there is no help. His breath goeth forth, he returneth to his earth; in that very day his thoughts perish. Happy is he that hath the God of Jacob for his help, whose hope is in the LORD his God:*
> Psa. 146:3-5

Consider the contrast between two kings of Judah: the first was Hezekiah, whom God told to prepare for death, but he repented, turned his face to the wall and wept and prayed. When he did so, God was touched and sent Isaiah to the king to tell him He had *seen his tears* and *heard his prayers*, and would heal him.

> *Go, and say to Hezekiah, Thus saith the LORD, the God of David thy father, I have heard thy prayer, I have seen thy tears: behold, I will add unto thy days fifteen years.*　　　　　　　　Isa. 38:5

The other king was Asa, who after experiencing the miracle power of God, did not look to Him when he became ill, but instead turned elsewhere with a tragic result.

> *And Asa in the thirty and ninth year of his reign was diseased in his feet, until his disease was exceeding great: yet in his disease he **sought not to the LORD**, but to the physicians. And Asa slept with his fathers, and died in the one and fortieth year of his reign.*　　　　　　　2 Chr. 16:12-13

Notice the Holy Spirit's own commentary upon this situation – that Asa sought *not to the Lord*, but, instead, the physicians.

### Looking for Signs

We need to make the decision to place our trust in Jesus by faith, even before we see physical proof. He criticized some for wanting proof before believing.

> *Then said Jesus unto him, Except ye see signs and wonders, **ye will not believe**.*　　　　　John 4:48

181

## Ignorance: Not Possessing Our Possessions

Satan loves to get us spinning our wheels, like a car stuck in the mud. He often deceives us into searching for that which is *already* ours. Because of our lack of understanding, it is possible for us to have something, but not *know* that we have it! This can be true of healing as well as of any other spiritual gift. "To possess" is not the same as "to use," nor is it the same thing as "to practice or receive." For example, Timothy had a gift, but Paul had to encourage him in its use.

> *Wherefore I put thee in remembrance that thou stir up the gift of God, which is in thee by the putting on of my hands.*                    2 Tim. 1:6

To have something is not the same as to use it, or to be blessed by it. There was a story about an elderly woman, who lived in St. Louis, whom her neighbors thought was extremely poor. She lived in a state of near poverty, even to the point of eating dog food. However, when she died, they found a shoebox in her closet, which contained more than $160,000 in cash. She hadn't used it, perhaps, because she didn't choose to, or because of a "spirit of poverty," or perhaps she was mentally ill and didn't understand its value. Nonetheless, she possessed money but was denied the benefits of that which she might otherwise have enjoyed.

Jesus has provided great abundance for us, but we must learn how to utilize the blessings at our disposal, and to get what we possess out of the closet.

## "I Deserve Crippling Arthritis, Because I've Exercised too Much."

There is also a theology of "deserved sickness." A

young school teacher expressed this doubt, that she deserved her sickness, when she came for prayer. She explained that as a PE (Physical Education) teacher she had used her joints more than most people.

"Perhaps you have," I agreed, "but what about all the PE teachers who aren't crippled with arthritis? Haven't they exercised just as you have? And what about professional athletes, who either play or practice every day? Can you see how slyly Satan attempts to get us to accept our afflictions, and not to fight?"

## "I Attended a Healing Service, but Wasn't Healed."

Remember that faith is evidence of things *not seen*, in this case our own healing amidst those being healed. Faith is a strong theology that can be used to combat the bad theology based on sight and physical evidence. I, too, went to a Kathryn Kuhlman meeting without being healed, but I was blessed to see what occurred, and it built my faith. That is, there was a purpose in it, and God used it for my good and eventual healing.

Don't you think that some of the people who went out into the wilderness to see Jesus, or who joined the crowds seeking healing at the hands of Jesus, had *unsuccessfully* sought prayer before? Some of them, no doubt, had already exhausted all natural means of attaining wholeness, but were healed in a meeting with Jesus!

## Denial of Reality Is a Block

This block covers a wide spectrum of theology. On one end, there is the person who is in denial, simply refusing to believe that the condition is as bad as it appears, and thus refuses to face the facts. On the other end, there is a perverse form of denial which carries Christian Science overtones – denying that sickness even exists. There is a close relationship between the doctrine of "positive confession," the "power of mental will power" as the means of healing, and the theology of Christian Science.

Regrettably, there has been introduced into Christian thought a strong influence of Christian Science thinking, that of mind-over-matter and its concept of the denial of reality. If your mind is strong enough, this theology suggests, you can deny that reality and substitute for it another reality.

There is a valid place for positive confession, or **positively confessing what the Word says about us.** However, not "positive confession" as we've been carelessly taught, and certainly not the denial of reality.

The Lord, whom we serve, identified Himself as "the Way the Truth and the Life." When Jesus used the word *Truth*, what He literally was saying in the original text was *Reality*. Jesus says I am "Reality." Jesus would not have us live a lie. Satan is the god of *unreality*, and the god of untruth, the author of lies.

If, for example, I have a broken arm, my proper confession is not "My arm is not broken." For *we know it is* broken, we *can see that it is* broken, and so can the world see that it is broken. What I can properly confess is this: "I have a broken arm, as you can see, BUT my God is bigger than a broken arm, AND Jesus Christ heals broken arms!"

## Repetitious, Positive Confession.

Some Christians have begun to use positive confessions like a "mantra" or as an "Open, Sesame." They seem to think if they say something often enough, they will convince themselves, or God, and somehow make themselves eligible to be healed. For example, saying over and over, "My eyes are healed."

I do not wish to sound unkind or totally opposed to

positive confession, for I most certainly am not. There is a very valid truth in confessing, or speaking aloud, what the Word of God says about us, such as "Let the weak say, I am strong!"

The problematic aspect enters when one is merely encouraged to parrot a Scripture or phrase that has been meaningful for someone else. When I ask, "What Scripture has *God* given to you?" They again give me a blank look, because they have not found a promise from God's word for themselves.

If you seek God whole heartedly, He will quicken a *specific word* to you.

### Do You Fear Making a Negative Confession?

Satan will use any tool at his disposal to attempt to frustrate your attempt to get to Jesus for healing. He wants to block your efforts to reach Jesus. He often uses the doctrine that one must not "confess" or say anything negative against sincere believers. If, for example, he can get you to believe that you cannot make a "negative confession," then he might just as well have torn James 5 out of your Bible. Because, if you are unable to make a "negative confession," you cannot summon the elders to pray for your healing, since you cannot admit that you are sick! To say that "I am sick" is a negative confession. I have had numerous people come forward for prayer in meetings who were afraid to tell me their needs, because of this very doctrine.

### Girl Who Wanted "...neeemerr gummph"

A few years ago, at our Thursday night meeting, a young woman come forward to sit in the prayer chair. I asked why she wanted prayer. She said, "I'd like prayer for ...." and clamped her hand over her mouth.

I asked again, "What is it that you need?"

Again, all she could get out with her hand over her mouth was a muffled, "I...neeemerr gummph."

I said, "What's the problem you need prayer for?"

She finally said, "I can't say."

I asked, "Why? Are you afraid of making a negative confession?"

She replied, "Yes." And continued, "One pastor told me to say this, and another told me to do that, and the other person told me to do something else, and they said to pray for it once and not to pray again or I'd make God mad." And she sobbed, "I'm just so confused, I don't know what to do!"

Then she began to superstitiously recite certain Scriptures in a parrot-like fashion.

I interrupted her, "What does that mean?"

She said, "I don't know, but they told me if I said that enough times I'd be healed."

As mentioned before, some people offer Scripture to be used like a magic wand, or as a magic incantation that people are led to believe will heal them, if they'll just recite it often enough. This is in contrast to proclaiming Scripture to build one's faith in its promise.

Let's just consider briefly each of the problems encountered in the case of this young woman.

(1) She was in bondage to a **fear of making a negative confession.** This is not an uncommon problem, but bondage of any kind is not from God. Take for instance the following example.

### Large Group Bound by Negative Confession

Years ago I drove about five hours down to Tennessee to speak on a Saturday evening for a Full Gospel Business Men's Fellowship Meeting, and gave my testimony. When I finished, I gave an altar call for salvation, and then an altar call for healing, and as I usually do, asked first for anyone in pain.

The people looked at one another like they had never heard the word, "pain."

Again, I offered, "Anyone in pain…? Are any of you hurting…? Anyone sick…? Anyone in need…?"

Based on the size of the crowd, the odds were that more than a hundred people were in need, and that in a normal situation I would be praying for needs for between an hour and two hours with a group of that size. I was beginning to think I was having a bad dream. After I'd invited them without a response four or five times, finally I called the president of the organization over, and suggested, "Why don't you invite them, I don't seem to be able to get any action."

So he invited anyone that had a need for physical healing or with any condition to come forward for prayer. They gave him the same reaction, so he dismissed the meeting with a benediction.

After the people left, I was stupefied and sat down with the leaders and we discussed the situation, attempting to understand what had just happened, and why. The leaders couldn't understand this either and just kept shaking their heads. I shared with them that based on past experience, in a group of comparable size, I would have expected no less than fifteen people to have come forward initially, and probably after the first were healed, at least another thirty, as a minimum.

At about that point a woman came back into the meeting room looking rather sheepishly. Self-consciously she admitted, "I came here tonight to get prayer for my cancer. Would you still be willing to pray for me?"

I said, "Sure we will, but why didn't you come forward earlier. Have you been under the teaching that says 'you can't make a negative confession?'"

She again looked sheepish and lowering her head, replied simply, "Yes."

Before we had finished praying for her, another man came in with a serious problem and before we finished praying for him, another came in. Each of them was bound by the fear of a negative confession. God still managed to break through the mental bondage that these people had taken upon themselves. However, only these three came back for prayer. I grieved all the way home for the effective way that Satan had been able to use a distorted doctrine to keep those people from being open to receive what Jesus had died to provide for them, and had sent me to Tennessee to deliver to them.

You see how insidious a bad doctrine can be, when people are afraid to admit that they have a problem, or a need, or a sickness? That's one of Satan's masterstrokes. If Satan can keep us from asking to be healed, then on the basis of James' admonition, "Ye *have not* because you *ask not*," one cannot expect to receive. Doctrines of these kinds accomplish Satan's purposes and block various groups of saints from receiving the healing that God wants them to have.

## What About Positive Confession?

(2) The girl in our original case had also been asked to make **a denial of reality**. The logical corollary to not making a negative confession is to always make a **positive confession**, and that can be carried to excess also.

Now there is a valid place for positive confession. If indeed God quickens a word to your heart, that although you are blind, you're going to see, then you can stand on that. You can confess that and profess that, if God has quickened it to you as a *rhema*.

*Logos* and *rhema* are two different Greek words for "word" used in Scripture. The *Logos* is the Word of God, universally true for all people at all times. The *rhema* of God is a word spoken by God, heard and received, specifically for you – quickened to you, made alive to you by the Spirit.

### Don't Pray More Than Once

(3) Another problem we observe in the case of the girl was the fear that she **couldn't pray more than one time,** or else she would dishonor God.

There's a teaching in some Christian circles that if you pray more than one time, you will dishonor God or negate the faith of your first prayer. Let me offer two Scriptural refutations of that doctrine.

The first Scriptural rebuttal we have already seen in a different light: Paul himself prayed three times. So Paul, who is a pattern for us, prayed for something more than once (2 Cor. 12:8). There's nothing wrong with praying more than once. Paul encouraged us to **pray without ceasing** (1 Th. 5:17). Jesus told us to knock and keep on knocking, to ask and keep on asking, seek and keep on seeking (Mat. 7:7). That doesn't sound as if He would be offended, if we prayed more than once. As I understand it, if you've been prayed for once and you're still sick, you're still eligible for the ministry of James chapter 5.

The invalidity of this doctrine was further demonstrated to me through a personal experience. A number of years ago I spoke in the basement of a church in Missouri. (I've noticed that we always seem to do praying for healing down by the boiler, as it somehow isn't considered "respectable." In the early days, I didn't think healing would work, if you were more than an arm's length from the boiler.)

On this occasion, it was a cold winter's evening, and

after I'd given my testimony, we prayed for the healing of probably 30 or 40 people. Finally the last woman was in the prayer chair. She complained of a back condition from birth, but said, "I have to admit that I'm a skeptic."

As I later learned, she was raised by Christian Science parents and was just beginning to come into the full knowledge of Jesus Christ. (Incidentally, she is today a leader in the Bible Study Fellowship.)

That evening we prayed for her back. I held her feet; the Lord lengthened her short leg. She was better, but she still had pain in her back. We prayed a second time, she was even better, but still had minor pain. When we prayed a third time, she was healed – completely freed of pain!

Since she was the last person, and the hour was late, we dismissed with prayer and I headed for the corner to pick up my coat and hat. At about that point I saw a "raging bull" coming from one corner of the room with steam coming out of his ears and he shouted at me, "How dare you do that?"

Startled, I asked, "How dare I *do what*?"

He said, "How dare you pray *three times* for that woman?"

He continued, "I've read all the books on faith, and they all say you can't pray more than one time, or else you dishonor God, and your faith is no good."

The only answer I had for him that evening was, "Well, brother, it worked."

He said, "I know it worked, and that's why I'm so mad."

I usually learn more from my mistakes than I do from my successes, and a week later the Lord showed me the answer that I should have given him.

You recall that when Jesus ministered to the blind man, He took him outside Bethsaida and ministered to him. Jesus ministered once, and the man was able to see men "walking as trees." Then Jesus, whose faith was perfect, prayed a second time, and the man was able to see *all things clearly.*

So here we see another Scriptural account which refutes the doctrine that says you can only pray once. And this account involves Jesus Himself!

### "Whom Are You Glorifying with Your Mouth?"

The contrast in Scripture to the doctrine of "positive confession" is the practice of immersion in the promises of God, and the positive confession of the Word of God. Scripture reminds us that,

> *Death and life are in the power of the tongue: and they that love it shall eat the fruit thereof.*
> Prov. 18:21

Too many individuals when they become sick, develop an unholy obsession with their disease, and study all the possible treatments for it. Similar to the hypochondriac, they slip into a mode where all they can talk about are their symptoms, and possible medical solutions. This causes their focus to be on the problem, rather than upon the solution. I encourage such people to try to treat their affliction as a cut with a scab. By looking at the scab every day you do not speed your healing, nor do you build your faith for it to go away. The way scabs heal best is to forget about them. The same is true, in a spiritual sense, of all forms of sicknesses.

By devoting your attention to the sickness, handicap, or affliction, you are to that same degree not focusing your thoughts upon the *solution* – faith in Jesus, your Healer. Too much knowledge about your condition and the possible treatments can be counter-productive to faith.

## A Case of "Too Much Knowledge"

Peggy was a dear woman, who attended a number of our meetings in the early days. One day she called for an appointment for healing. When she arrived, she introduced her need by saying, "Bill, I have come in the past and had my back healed, and my eyes as well, but I'm really not sure that God can heal my teeth."

Curious, I asked, "Why should it be any more difficult for God to heal your teeth than to heal your back, or your eyes?"

She responded honestly, "Because I worked for years in a dentist's office as a dental assistant...and I know all the reasons why my teeth *shouldn't be healed.*"

She was wise enough to recognize a potential block to her faith: her knowledge would tend to get in the way of her faith to be healed!

If you want to devote time and study in connection with your affliction, why not spend that time studying God's word, and filling your mind with faith-building testimonies? When faced with a choice, instead of speaking negative thoughts, which are inspired by fear and doubt, try proclaiming Scripture that confirms and edifies your faith in the Lord's promises. These can be both general promises of healing or, as discussed, the specific revelations of healing provided to you through the ministry of the Holy Spirit (personal words of wisdom, knowledge, or even prophecies).

Recall the Israelites who, when confronted by the giants in the land, reported *"We were in our own sight as grasshoppers..."* (Num. 13:33). Contrast their fear-filled reaction with that of David, who looked at Goliath and mentally compared Goliath, not with himself, but with His God, and challenged him with these words:

*Thou comest to me with a sword, and with a spear, and with a shield: but I come to thee in the name of the LORD of hosts, the God of the armies of Israel, whom thou hast defied.*                          1 Sam. 17:45

### "Has Satan Been Lying to You?"

Satan speaks to us through the voice of bad theology expressing negative thoughts in our minds, such as,

"I deserve my afflictions because...

"I brought this upon myself by too much drinking, smoking, eating, exercise, etc."

"I'm not good enough for God to heal me."

"I'm not important enough."

"I don't know enough Scripture."

"I'm too great a sinner, I've sinned too much, too many times."

"God wants me sick."

"I didn't take care of my body in my youth."

"I haven't always eaten the right foods."

"I don't like that man's healing ministry."

"I refuse to accept the possibility of needing deliverance."

"I'm afraid to go forward for prayer in a meeting."

"God is teaching me something."

"God is punishing me for...

> ...not praying enough
>
> ...not reading the Bible enough"

"He is denying me healing, because I haven't fasted enough."

"I've already been prayed for by my elders and it didn't work."

The preceding and any other rationalizations are invalid reasons to accept your sickness and condition. They are lies of the enemy, examples of bad theology, and are Satan's selling points to try to get you to accept your sickness or condition, without resisting or fighting it. They are his means of keeping you from the healing power of Jesus, and are designed to prevent you from wholeheartedly seeking your healing. Each one, I might add, may be countered through Scriptural promises and Scriptural evidence!

### "Have You Refused to Accept God's Method of Ministering to You?"

Some tend to be unteachable – they stubbornly hold on to their bad theology and refuse to listen to correct theology. For instance, they think they know all they need to know about God, or His plans for healing, and are thus unwilling to accept something that is new to them, or that doesn't agree with their personal "theology."

You may recall the story of Naaman, and the instructions received by Elisha.

> *Elisha sent a messenger to say to him [Naaman], "Go, wash yourself seven times in the Jordan, and your flesh will be restored and you will be cleansed."*
>
> 2 Kings 5:10

What if Naaman had refused to accept the "new" prescription of dipping in the Jordan seven times, offered to him by Elijah? God works sometimes in mysterious ways.

### "But God is Sovereign."

Indeed He is, and because He is, He has the sovereign right to heal you and to be a Healer! As mentioned in Chapter 10, He in fact *chooses* to heal, and He does so repeatedly, as His Word bears testimony. There are some who would attempt to use God's sovereignty as an argument against healing. They would argue that because God is sovereign, He must in some way be causing your sickness.

However, God is sovereignly good, and He is not sovereignly schizophrenic. He cannot, on the one hand be described as "light, in Him there is no darkness in Him at all," while on the other hand be a cruel inflictor of pain and suffering. That would be the combination of light and darkness, or good and evil. Such individuals who teach that both exist in the nature of God are confused, and quite frankly have *a form of godliness, but deny the power thereof.* From such a man we are told to *"turn away."* (2 Tim. 3:5) These men are attempting to excuse their own powerlessness, by implying that God is fickle and sometimes doesn't want to heal.

### The Theology of Inner Healing.

Many of the concepts used in inner-healing are rooted in the theology of reincarnation, and perhaps the best known technique is having people regress or "go back" into their past lives. They tell a subject, "You are now age 5, you're 4, you're 3," just as many do in the Christian version of "inner-healing." They continue, "You are 5, 4, 3, you're now age 0, or age 0 minus 9 months," depending on the style of inner-healing utilized. The difference is that those involved in reincarnation do not stop at age 0, they go further, "You are now minus 10 years, minus 5 years; you're dying, how are you dying?"

The person may respond that he has been injured in an auto accident on an icy road and is "trapped under the car, I'm freezing to death on the side of the road." It is obvious to any Christian, that the voice responding to such questions cannot be that of the individual describing a former life. Rather, it is a demon speaking through him.

Now the danger inherent in what is called "Christian

inner-healing" becomes evident, if it employs the same methodology. If a demon can answer an inquiry at minus age 10, then I submit to you that a demon can, likewise, respond at age plus 10 years or 5 years or 3 years, as a person regresses. Another major problem with "Christian" inner-healing is that it usually involves taking a subject back and not merely "reliving a painful incident", but also brings Jesus into the equation. For example, your father beat you with a club when you were a child, and broke your arm in the process. When you submit to "Christian" inner-healing, the counselor takes you back to that event, but this time you are asked to visualize Jesus coming upon the situation, taking the club out of your father's hand, and loving you both, so that you and your father reconcile on the spot. That sounds nice, but realize it is an *attempt to replace the truth with a lie!* In point of fact, your father did not stop beating you, Jesus did not take the club out of his hand, your arm was still broken. Reality is reality! You will still need to forgive your father.

We have had many people come for healing or deliverance that had previously been through such "inner-healing" sessions, and found their problems remained or worsened. It is important to ask the person who offers "Christian inner-healing" what they mean by that term, since it is not a Scriptural phrase. There are some who inadvertently use the term to cover valid repentance, confession, deliverance and healing, but it is a very nebulous term and there are almost as many variations as there are practitioners.

### Relying upon Gimmicks and Fad Doctrines
Some of the crazy doctrines that have infiltrated Christian circles would be almost ludicrous and laughable, if it weren't for the fact that people actually believed them, and acted upon them.

In the very early days of the Charismatic movement, in 1972, I attended a large conference in Anaheim, California, wanting to learn more about the moving of the Spirit. At that time there was a popular, yet screwy doctrine to the effect that "If you will *smash your glasses in faith* (apparently as a sign of your faith) God will heal your eyes." I know of dozens of people in our area who did, in fact, smash their glasses.

I must confess the doctrine sounded pretty flaky to me, but I determined to be open minded. Surprisingly, when I arrived at the conference, one of the featured speakers was a minister, who later wrote a book on the practice.

After listening to this fellow teach this dubious doctrine in the morning session for an hour or so (remember I was then a babe – a newly Spirit-filled believer), I happened to run into him at a break later in the day. I'm sure he didn't recognize me, when I asked, "Say, how are *your* eyes?"

He responded, "Oh, I still can't see a darned thing."

Can you believe that? Here was a guy out on the circuit with a following, and people were paying money to have him come and teach his screwy doctrine.

How ridiculous (and hypocritical) to be advocating and teaching a principle that had not been proven to work.

\* \* \*

If you have seen blocks in this chapter that you feel relate to you, you might start your prayer:

*DearLord, I thank you for Your truth, which sets me free! Forgive me for falling prey to or believing any of the enemy's lies or distortions....*

* * *

I trust I'm  free of those problems,  but there may be
something else....

# Chapter 14

# "Could You Have a Pride Block?"

### Pride Is a Block

It should not come as a surprise that pride can block the blessings of God in our lives. Pride can, for instance, resist the need to ask for prayer to be healed. Pride exists, but what is surprising for most of us is that we ourselves may be exhibiting forms of pride and similar resistance to God, even if we are unaware.

Pride comes in union with a number of other issues, like rebellion. Rebellion may say, "I don't have to ask," or "I don't need to ask," or "I deserve it and He owes it to me." Pride also brings with it fear of embarrassment, or fear of loss of personal dignity. And pride can come in many forms, including both religious and denominational types.

### Do You Have A Parochial Pride Block?

When asked by a non-immediate family member to visit one of their sick relatives, many times the immediate family has turned me away from the hospital room refusing to allow me to pray for their relative. Typically they have said, "We have *our own* priest, minister, etc." As a result, for nearly thirty years, I have not made a hospital call unless specifically invited by the sick person, or by an immediate family member. This kind of response throws up a block to the ministry of the Holy Spirit.

## "I've Been Prayed for by the Elders
## at *My* Church."

I recall one man telling me this with a degree of stubborn pride, and I grieved for him. I knew that, in this case, his church did not truly believe that it is God's will to heal. In fact his church was experiencing an epidemic of cancer, oddly enough, after the minister and his family succumbed to that disease (due, I believe, to some occult influences operating in and around the church).

Your elders have prayed. That's is encouraging, but are you well? Do they really believe that God wills to heal today? And have they submitted to the power of the Holy Spirit in their own lives? Are they merely 'elders' in name only, in a church that does not believe in healing. All men do not have the same level of faith.

And as another unfortunate possibility, some elders are not stalwarts in the kingdom. As an example, I served as an elder at a mainline denominational church many years ago, and had not received any valid teaching on how to minister effectively to the sick. We later learned one of the other elders was a Theosophist (one who claims to possess knowledge of God through philosophical reasoning, and denies the need for salvation through the blood of Jesus). I know of another church where one of the elders owned abortion parlors. Such men cannot possibly be in one accord with true Christian elders.

The point is this: do not be limited strictly to your own church! The body of Christ is national, and international. And there are ministry gifts administered throughout.

## Have You Humbled Yourself?

*God resisteth the proud, but giveth grace unto the humble.*                                       James 4:6b

*Humble yourselves therefore under the mighty hand of God, that he may exalt you in due time*

1 Pet. 5:6

Another problem we have observed involves the person who comes without humility – or who comes without repentance. Several years ago, when AIDS first began to be an epidemic, a homosexual was brought to me by his mother. When I asked if he was willing to repent of his sinful behavior, He said, "No."

I said, "Well are you willing to repent of your homosexuality?"

"No."

He was unwilling to accept God's assessment of homosexuality as sin (Lev. 20:13, Rom 1:26, 27), or to repent, and was unwilling to humble himself before God. He was, instead, belligerently demanding healing on his own terms, thinking that I was some guy with a magic wand whom his mother told him was able to heal him of AIDS. Even though he acknowledged that his homosexual activity had brought about, or had been the precipitating cause of his contracting AIDS, he remained adamant, and refused to repent or to humble himself before God.

He was really not ready to become a candidate for healing prayer.

## Presumptive Pride

I can tell you first hand that when someone comes to you in ministerial pride and attempts to condemn you for being sick, it is the farthest thing from the ministry of Jesus. Once, as I was sniffling with a cold and working in our Christian bookstore, a man walked in who commented, "How long are you going to be dumb enough to keep that cold before you *ask me* to pray for you?"

I thought, "I need this guy, like I need another cold." He wasn't from our fellowship and didn't know me well enough to address me like that. His tone also suggested pride in his ministerial gifts. It is clear that his frame of mind was set, that healing was something from *him*, and that all you had to do was let *him* pray for it. His thinking was that anybody who was sick was stupid. How tragic, inconsiderate, and uncompassionate.

He suffered from religious pride.

Along these lines, there is a unique aspect of pride in the area of religion and presumptive familiarity with the things of God. We cover this next.

## Any Doctrine Which Is out of Balance Can Become Demonic

Any doctrine that moves out of balance with the Word of God can, and will, be used by Satan to cause harm and to deceive. The effect for some Christians is blindness to the total goodness of God and to His ability and willingness to heal. Often these doctrines try to limit God.

Recognize also that we are considering here excesses and perversions, abuses or warping of Scriptures. This absolutely does not advocate discarding all of the concepts we're discussing. Abuses of the things of God do not make God or His ministerial gifts any less real or valid.

## Religious Blocks

We have covered, in abundance, the theological blocks to healing from the mainstream denominations. Now it is time to turn our attention to the churches which are pursuing the modern ministry of Jesus Christ through the power of the Holy Spirit.

## "We Know All There Is about Healing."

On one occasion I was praying for healing in a Spirit-filled church. After I had prayed for a woman to be healed, she began a war dance, apparently trying to convince everyone that she had been touched by the Lord. When I quietly asked her to stop dancing, and to check to see if the symptoms of the sickness were indeed gone, she took affront. Glaring at me out of anger-filled eyes, she snorted, "I know *all* about healing. I have been healed *many times.*"

An old Pentecostal pastor once told me that he felt "the hardest people to get healed were Pentecostal people."

"Why should that be," I wondered? In retrospect, I think there are several reasons:

1.) Some individuals have simply become accustomed to going through the motions of being prayed for, and wanting to appear "spiritual." Likewise they may be merely pretending to be healed

2.) For others, it has become almost a ritual or a game to go through the 'healing line' in order to 'not miss a blessing.'

3.) Some have fallen into a habit of trying to help out the pastor, and not wanting him to look bad. They have developed a habit of always saying, "I'm healed," whether anything has actually happened to them or not.

4.) Some are victims of pride and think they know all there is to know about healing. ("We've had healing in our church for years!")

5.) For some others their denominational 'knowledge' and traditions have simply gotten in their way. One major block to ministry in such churches is the refusal to believe that Christians can be afflicted by demons. And demons are often the source of sickness, as Jesus demonstrated in His ministry.

## Need to Be Still Before the Lord

Many times I found that the people for whom I was attempting to pray were so busy praying, e.g. praying in tongues, praising the Lord with arms uplifted, or performing a variety of other religious activities, that it was difficult for me to even get a word in. I have often come away frustrated after attempting to conduct healing services in situations of this kind, and rarely saw the kind of results we saw in other churches.

The Spirit has difficulty operating where there is a lack of order; likewise chaotic environments are hard for humans to operate in. There is a time to let fear go, to allow the person praying to do his work, and to be still before the awesome presence of God.

I repeatedly sought the Lord on this matter, knowing that this sort of thing "ought not so to be." Finally the Lord graciously gave me an illustration to use with such people, and it has really helped explain the problem. He told me to tell them from His Word, "Be still, and know that I am God," (Psa. 46:10) and then tell them about the working of a CB radio.

I now simply and lovingly relate to them the understanding that the Lord has given to me. The Lord has shown me that very often we Charismatic and/or Pentecostal people have been taught that we need to do certain things in order to get healed. We've been told to 'say we are healed,' to 'claim it,' to 'confess it,' to 'thank Jesus for it in advance,' to 'praise Jesus for our healing,' to 'pray in tongues,' or to 'raise our hands in praise.'

There is a proper time and place for doing all of those things, but this isn't the time. Now He would say unto you simply, "Be still, and know that I am God."

There is a time to minister *to the Lord*, and a time to receive *from the Lord*. This is a time to be still, and to receive from Him!  Peter said, "Lord, you're not going to wash my feet."  The Lord told Him that if He didn't allow Him to wash his feet, that he would have no part in the ministry.

We, like Peter, feel we should be washing His feet, but He wants us, instead, to let Him minister *to us*.

I then tell them how the Lord made this very clear to me and gave me the example of the CB Radio.  You know how they operate: you push down a button to talk, and you release it to receive messages.  So long as the transmit button is down, you can't hear the other party: you cannot receive while the transmit (send) button is down.

We Charismatic and Pentecostal people all too often hold the button down, and do all the talking: trying to tell God what needs to be done, and how He should do it.  He already knows more about us, and our conditions than we do.  He would have us take our thumbs off the "send button," so that we might receive from Him.

He knows how to heal us without any advice or assistance from us.  Now all you need to do is simply relax, and breathe.  Let Him do all the rest.  Be still, bask in His presence, and breathe in His healing power...Now just receive from Him!

There is a time to be still and let Him be God, to let Him "transmit"...Be still and receive!

\* \* \*

If you have seen blocks in this chapter that you feel relate to you, you might start your prayer:

*Lord,  please forgive me for any pride that may have crept in,  and teaach me to be still and let You work.*
\* \* \*
"What else might be blocking me?"

# Chapter 15

# Blatant Sin Blocks Healing

*But let a man examine himself...*          1 Cor 11:28a

### "Do I Have A Sin Block?"

Sin can be a block to healing. This is not always the case, as there is always a complex mix of reasons for the sickness that plagues mankind. However, that there are "sin blocks" to healing is a self-evident principle. One of the reasons for blocked prayer is found in Jeremiah:

> *Your iniquities have turned away these things, and* ***your sins have withholden good things*** *from you.*
>
>                                                  Jer. 5:25

Note that "iniquities" have prevented the person in this passage from receiving the blessings, which God intended for him or her, the "good things" of God. Sin is throwing a block!   This reminds us of our discussion on Job, where the Devil had an upper hand because of the inherent sinful nature of man, prior to the sacrifice of Jesus Christ. Let's look at Isaiah chapter 59 and we'll see this principle re-stated.

> *Behold, the LORD'S hand is not shortened, that it cannot save; neither his ear heavy, that it cannot hear: But your iniquities have separated between you and your God, and* ***your sins have hid his face*** *from you, that he will not hear.*          Isa 59:1-2

Isaiah agrees with the sin principle as stated above, and emphasizes that God's face and ears are hidden from us by our sins. There appears to be two actions taking place in this sense: God hides his face from our sin, and Satan takes advantage of an open door. Read the entire chapter for context and to also see the promise of hope. But make no mistake, disobedience in any form is an affront to God, and an opportunity for Satan.

This principle, of action and reaction can best be explained through an illustration the Lord once provided me, the *umbrella of God*

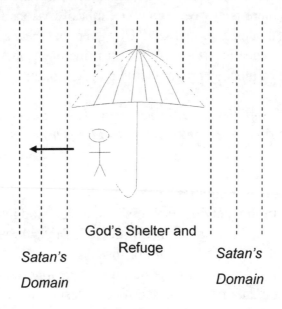

God's Shelter and Refuge

Satan's Domain

Satan's Domain

Notice that when we accept Jesus, we are covered by the righteousness and shield of our Savior. He is our armor (Eph. 6:11), or as this picture shows, our umbrella. When we willfully step out from under the umbrella, through sin, we temporarily leave the refuge of Jesus and enter a domain of unrighteousness. This is Satan's domain. And this is when all trouble breaks loose.

Note, most importantly, that it is not God's will for us to leave His shelter, just as it is not His will for us to sin. As such, it is also not His will for us to become afflicted in any way by the satanic storm raging outside. The person leaves of his own accord, in his own will. Note also that this is not a loss of salvation, but merely a temporary "disturbance" in our walk with the Lord. He is still faithful to us.

"Temporary" implies that this is only a matter of timing, because there is an open door of repentance. Thankfully, we have a Savior, Jesus, who intercedes for us 24 hours a day, 7 days a week in the Holiest of Holies in heaven. He invites us back under the umbrella and back under His protection, and even more, causes *all things to work together for our good.* This is part of the incredible inheritance we have through our salvation in Him. He makes even our darkest hour into a miracle. This image is supported by Scripture, the most powerful and touching, being Psalm 107, a Psalm that provides hope to those who are afflicted, because of their sin.

> *Some became fools through their rebellious ways **and suffered affliction because of their iniquities**. They loathed all food and drew near the gates of death. Then they cried to the LORD in their trouble, and he saved them from their distress. **He sent forth his word and healed them**; he rescued them from the grave. Let them give thanks to the LORD for **his unfailing love and his wonderful deeds for men**. Let them sacrifice thank offerings and tell of his works with songs of joy.* Ps 107:17-22

God "sends forth His Word," brings them back under His umbrella, and "heals them!"

## What is Your Unique Disobedience?

Your disobedience may be different from anyone else's disobedience. If God has told you to do something, and you are not doing it, that's disobedience. God may not have said the same thing to anyone else, but if He has spoken it to you, you need to be obedient.

We are so prone to make laws out of things. At some point in the past, God apparently told a particular woman that *for her* to wear make-up and certain kinds of apparel would be a form of harlotry. So she ceased wearing make-up, put her hair up in a bun and spread the word that this is the way to dress to be holy.

Your manner of dress is an external. God is concerned with modesty, but more so modesty of the heart. The heart can remain unchanged in spite of external apparel.

In the introduction, I stated that there can be as many different blocks as there are people. Once the Lord impresses you to do, or to refrain from doing something, then to not obey is rebellion against the Lord. We want to avoid rebellion and disobedience in every form, and to be as right as possible with God.

There is a principal here. Disobedience in any form can be a block. The key word is "can," meaning it is a possibility, but not a hard fast rule. The reason I say this is because God normally deals directly with man's disobedience, to convict him before matters get out of hand. Only when man becomes too hard of heart, too proud, too corrupt, does he effectively move out from under the protection of the umbrella and expose himself to the storms raging outside God's will (1 Cor. 5:5).

As an example – we were all witnesses to the TV scandals in the Church. God warned those men long before the situations got out of hand. I know this by faith, from knowing how God deals with His own men in general. And I know it personally, because a man from our fellowship was invited to go to work for P.T.L. more than twenty years prior to the scandals. He refused to accept a position with them and told them that the reason for his refusal was that he believed they were "an accident waiting to happen," because of the way they handled their funds.

I believe that, when sick, most of us will run through a personal laundry list of possible areas of disobedience and sin. This is a good first step and may be a necessary part of the humbling process that leads up to healing, as it positions us to receive strictly out of the goodness and compassion of Jesus Christ (and not our own righteousness).

One thing that most of us tend to overlook is our finances. Have we been obedient to God in regard to our money, and our tithing?

### "Have I Robbed God?"

One reason some Christians have not received their healing may be due to the fact that they have not been obedient in the area of their finances. Again, not a hard and fast rule, but a possibility. Can a man rob God? Apparently so, as Malachi indicates:

> *Bring ye all the tithes into the storehouse, that there may be meat in mine house, and prove me now herewith, saith the LORD of hosts, if I will not open you the windows of heaven, and pour you out a blessing, that there shall not be room enough to receive it. And I will rebuke the devourer for your sakes, and he shall not destroy the fruits of your ground; neither shall your vine cast her fruit before the time in the field, saith the LORD of hosts.* Mal. 3:10-11

Seeking first the kingdom of God includes surrendering the hold on your money and providing a tithe to His kingdom. We need to get as right as possible with God, especially as we are seeking a healing.

Sickness is a disorder of the natural processes of the body. One naturally begins to search himself when sick, to see if there might be an area of disobedience: "Have I forgiven everyone?" "Am I harboring anything against anyone?" "Have I sinned?" "What might I have done, or be doing, that could be displeasing to God."

Jesus made a wonderful promise predicated upon wholehearted devotion to God:

> But seek ye first the kingdom of God, and his righteousness; and **all these things** shall be added unto you. Mat. 6:33

And "all these things shall be added unto you" would include any needed healings.

It is imporant to remember also, that man will never be forgotten, nor forsaken by God. This is a promise from Jesus.

> I will never leave thee, nor forsake thee. Heb 13:5

However, while man does remain a Covenant child of God, he is still permitted to eat the fruit of his doings; to endure the results of any evil ways; to reap the pain, suffering, sorrow and shame brought upon himself by his own erroneous choices. Man has the free will to walk outside the umbrella.

## "Am I Guilty of Idolatry?"
## "Could I Be Rebellious?"

Rebellion is a very common problem. As an example, a woman asked me why she couldn't get her prayers answered. One reason that struck me was because her pastor is a thief. He doesn't pay his bills, and people as far away as the next state know about him. He is a man that does not honor his word.

And yet she has chosen to remain in a false church, or a church in error. Remaining wasn't an act of rebellion for her until the Lord showed her the error, and told her to leave. Once she knew that her place of worship was a false church, once she knew it was corrupt, then it became rebellious to remain. She admitted to me that she knew in her heart that the pastor was wrong, and *knew* she was supposed to leave.

## Diseased with ALS

Recently an ALS (commonly known as Lou Gehrig's disease) patient related to me how her condition hit her shortly after a divorce. She went on to relate that she went for prayer at her church and asked them to pray for peace.

I pointed out to her, that the primary desire of her heart was for peace, because her problem was *dis-ease*. She had a lack of peace, no ease in her soul from the torment of her problems and this *dis-ease* had contributed towards, or opened a door for her physical disease!

Oftentimes we find that the root of a physical problem lies inward. People who are dis-eased in their spirits (p.e., tormented with unforgiveness or bitterness over a real or perceived wrong) are vulnerable to disease, as *even the medical profession has noted*. One often finds this inward torment working itself outward into a manifestation in the physical body.

## An Abortion Block

God can forgive anything that is repented of and con- fessed to Him. However, there are certain specific areas of unconfessed sins that can be blocks to healing, sins such as abortion. This particular sin is a combination of sins, in- cluding the sin of abortion and the sin of murder. In our book Ministering To Abortion's Aftermath, we offer a dozen testimonies of healings and instantaneous miracles which resulted once the abortion issue was fully dealt with.

## Generic Sin Blocks as Indicated by James

In addition to abortion, there are other things that can be sin blocks to healing that are clearly implied.

*Is any sick among you? let him call for the elders of the church; and let them pray over him, anointing him with oil in the name of the Lord: And the prayer of faith shall save the sick, and the Lord shall raise him up; and **if he have committed sins**, they shall be forgiven him. Confess your faults one to another, and pray one for another, that ye may be healed.*
James 5:14-16

We should notice, it says, "If he have committed sins, they shall be forgiven him." We cannot overlook the connection made in verse 15, between sin and sickness. In verse 16 James encourages us to *confess our faults* one to another, in order that *we may be healed.*

Clearly, James teaches that sins of various types can be either causes of sickness, or blocks to healing, as we have already seen. Thus the importance of confessing our faults is extremely important.

## Might You Have an Unforgiveness Block?

Years ago I was invited to speak in a hospital in St. Louis. Several years before this, I spoken there and the man now in charge of the meeting had been healed of emphysema. They had arranged folding chairs in the cafeteria in a big circle, with several narrow aisles each two feet wide, leading to the center.

A crowd began straggling into the room until there were probably over two hundred people seated. I was seated in the front with my brother, who happened to be the purchasing director for the hospital, waiting for the meeting to start. It was then that we noticed two men dragged a young girl in for prayer. They were half-dragging, half-carrying her, each of them supporting her one of her arms. Her head flopped from side to side, her arms flopped, her ankles dragged on the floor, and she obviously was in very bad shape. Struggling, they finally got her into a chair in the front row.

My brother leaned over and commented, "Oh what a tragic case. That must be a birth defect, multiple sclerosis or muscular dystrophy."

Our observations were interrupted as they began introducing me. After my testimony, we started praying for healing, and saw the Lord begin to mightily heal people. Very shortly, the friends commenced struggling, trying to get the crippled girl to her feet. I stopped them saying, "Let's wait a little bit, and let the Lord build our faith, before we pray for this young lady."

So a little later, after she had seen a lot of other people dramatically healed, and we were down to the most serious cases, I told her friends, "Now, bring her on up."

So they put her in the prayer chair, and I asked her, "What has caused you to be in the shape you are in?"

She replied, "I was in a car wreck."

Incredulous, I asked, "A car wreck? How did it happen?"

She said, "Well I was in the back seat of a car, and we hit a truck head on." She continued, "I was just torn to pieces. I've had five operations, and they can't do anything more for me. This is the best they can do: to have me in a shape like this, where I can't even walk."

"Have you forgiven the people that caused the accident?" I inquired.

She looked me right in the eye and said, "Hell, no!"

I had to give her an 'A' for honesty. I then asked, "Why haven't you?"

She said, "If somebody had done this to you, could you forgive them?"

I responded, "Well I don't know that I could, but I know that you *need to*." I pursued the issue, "How did the accident happen?"

Devoid of emotion, she recounted, "I was in the back seat of the car. The guy in the back seat with me was drunk. The guy and his date in the front seat were also both drunk."

Now, of course, this is her version of the story – *they* were all drunk, she was sober. Anyway, the guy in the back seat tried to rape her. She said she kicked up such a ruckus, the guy in the front seat turned around to see what was happening in the back seat, and ran head on into the truck. The car was totally demolished, the other three drunks got out of the car without a scratch, while she was torn to pieces.

Gesturing at her mangled body, she continued, "They did this to me."

And then as people often want to do, she tried to do a little 'wheeling and dealing' with God. She asked point blank, "Now, can you guarantee me I'll walk out of here if I do forgive those people?"

I answered, "Well no, I can't guarantee that you will, but I can pretty well guarantee you that, if you don't, you won't."

She still wasn't yet willing to forgive them. So, I said, "Well you just sit there and watch while we pray for some more people."

So we prayed about another half hour for other people, and finally I turned back to her and asked, "Now, are you ready to forgive those people?"

She said, "Well I'll try, if you'll help me."

They got her back in the prayer chair, and I explained forgiveness to her: that there are three natural steps to accomplish forgiveness, and one supernatural step. The three natural steps are our responsibility. We have to first of all confess the unforgiveness as sin, because that's how God views it. Second, we must renounce the sin of unforgiveness. And then third, we then must make the decision with our mind, confess it with our mouth, preferably in the presence of a witness, to forgive that person or those persons who have hurt us or wronged us.

Having done these three natural steps, we can rightfully expect the Lord to do the fourth, the supernatural step, and take away the pain, the hurt, all the poison out of the relationships and to heal.

I led her in a prayer, and then she prayed and forgave the guy in the front seat that caused the accident; the date that was drunk and tried to rape her; the doctors who had messed her up and caused her all the pain, and left her unable to walk; as well as all the people who had criticized her and had been unable to help her.

Having forgiven them all, we then prayed for her healing...and she stood up out of the prayer chair! I took her by the arm, and said, "Let's try walking." So we walked around the chair in which she had been sitting.

After one lap around the chair, she looked at me and asked, "Am I walking, or are you walking me?"

I said, "I'm just holding your arm to steady you a bit."

She said, "Let me try it." So she took one more lap around the prayer chair on her own. Then she started heading for the narrow center aisle.

I asked, "Where are you going? Are you going to try an obstacle course?"

She said determinedly, "Nope. I am going home!" Apparently calling to a friend, announced "Mary, get my purse, we're leaving!"

She walked out of the hospital that night under her own power: a tremendous testimony to the power of God to heal, when the block of unforgiveness was removed.

* * *

If you have seen blocks in this chapter that you feel relate to you, you might start your prayer:

*Lord Jesus, I thank You for the demonstrations of Your power and rejoice over these testimonies of Your healing virtue lovingly poured out upon Your people. Forgive me for any and all sin blocks I may have acquired, and let me receive Your fullness.*

* * *

In addition to those blocks resulting from our own wrong decisions, there may be blocks from the occult of which we may be unaware...

# Chapter 16

# Unsuspected Blocks
# From The Occult

An unusual but powerful block is found in the following account. I have encountered several similar cases, which required the destruction of an object which held occult power and prevented freedom and healing.

### Rural Faith Healer

Many times you will hear accounts of people claiming to have been healed as a result of being taken when they were direly ill to a rural "faith-healer," who sprinkled swamp water on them, or mumbled over them and they were healed.

Derek Prince told me the story of a young girl brought to him for healing of a chronic condition. He happened to notice an amulet that she was wearing around her neck as a pendant. He asked her about the amulet, because he had an uneasy feeling about it.

She told him that as a girl of twelve, she'd had an incurable disease. Relatives had taken her to a rural faith healer, an old lady out in the country, who was probably a witch or at the very least a charmer, and she mumbled over her. She then rubbed her body and put the amulet around her neck and told her to wear it. "So long as you wear it," the lady said, "you'll stay well."

Derek and the young girl cracked the amulet open and found inside a little piece of rolled up paper on which these words were written,

> *"Dear Satan,*
> *Keep this child alive and well,*
> *Until her soul roasts in hell."*

We may make light of things like this, and dismiss them as merely harmless games, but make no mistake, **they are deadly serious.**

The girl was then led through a prayer which renounced both the amulet and the previous occult healing. All ties were broken with the witch who had manipulated her previously. And then, she was healed anew and afresh.

Another extremely insidious block that we have encountered involves the demonic doctrine of reincarnation.

## Reincarnation Block

Once after a typical morning service at the mainline denominational church we attended years ago, Sue and I were approached by a desperate young mother. She tearfully begged us to come to her home that evening to pray for her son, who had a terminal brain tumor. When we arrived, we were met at the front door by the same woman. She greeted us brusquely saying, "I'm not going to let you come in. I don't want you to pray for my child."

Shocked, I asked, "Why not? This morning you begged us to come."

She explained her reasoning, "Well one of the other elders from your church came by this morning, and explained *reincarnation* to us. I now realize that my son is being punished for something he did in a former lifetime, and that if he were to be healed, he'd have to come back and go through this again," she began to cry. Continuing, she said, "I just couldn't put him through all this again."

I'm ashamed to admit that we were unable to convince her to let us in to pray for her child.

You see how effectively even the rather stupid blocks, that Satan instigates, work to prevent individuals from seeking Jesus for their healing. This is also illustrative of the un-enlightenment that can exist within orthodox Christianity in our day.

There is something of which we need to be aware and to remind ourselves repeatedly. And that is compassion, and the need to be compassionate. When we see a crippled or afflicted person, we want to be careful not to imply or even to think that the person has been afflicted due to a great sin, or because in some way they're greater sinners than we are. Tragically, that mentality does creep into the Church and is baseless.

There may even be a generational aspect to an illness, even crippling. The sins of the ancestors may be bearing down upon the body of a completely innocent person. For example, a woman whose mother, or grandmother had abortions could find herself unable to conceive a child, as a result of this ancestral sin. This would be a form of a "generational curse." [A direct curse of this kind (however, non-ancestral) is seen in operation upon the family of Abimelech in Genesis 20:17-18.]

Furthermore, there may have been some vulnerable point, whether in the womb or as a child, where the Devil struck with his fury. I pray that all those who are so maimed would come to know the Lord Jesus Christ as their healer.

There is a passage in Deuteronomy, with which many are unfamiliar, that forbids certain activities for the people of God.

# Occult Involvement Blocks

*When thou art come into the land which the LORD thy God giveth thee, thou shalt not learn to do after the abominations of those nations. There shall not be found among you any one that maketh his son or his daughter to pass through the fire, or that useth divination, or an observer of times, or an enchanter, or a witch, Or a charmer, or a consulter with familiar spirits, or a wizard, or a necromancer.*

Deut. 18:9-11

God Himself considers the things which He lists to be abominations before Him, and forbids them for His people. His list includes, One who makes "his son or his daughter to pass through the fire," which would be referred to today as infant sacrifice, or abortion.

One "that useth divination," would be those who attempt to "divine" the future, or gain guidance through consulting fortune-tellers, palm-readers, ESP, Tarot cards, Ouija boards, readers of tea-leaves, or similar forms of occult guidance. Any attempt to attain information that God in His wisdom has not chosen to grant to us would fit into this or the following categories.

One who is "an observer of times," is one who, in an attempt to fathom the unknown, or learn secret things, would consult horoscopes, astrology,etc. "Enchanters", are those who "cast spells" or "enchant" individuals. A hypnotist would fall under this heading. (So would the rural faith healer described earlier in this Chapter.) "Witches" are those who seek to get another to do their bidding (or will) by utilizing a power other than the Holy Spirit; the power that enables them to exercise their will over that of another is, nonetheless, from Satan.

A "charmer," is also one who cast spells, but usually uses "charms" or amulets. A "consulter with familiar spirits." Today these agents of Satan are referred to as "mediums" or as "channelers." "Familiar spirits" are either those one can get familiar with, or those who are familiar with you, because they have been associated with your family for many years (or in some cases for generations).

A "channeler" is one who allows demons to speak through him/her. All practitioners of the black arts, are fobidden, including witches, warlocks (male witch), sorcerers and wizards, or and who cast of spells.

The term "necromancer," is probably the least familiar to the modern reader. A necromancer is one who attempts to contact the dead, by means of "seances," trances, and the like. Of course, it is obviously not actually the dead, but demons which are contacted.

* * *

If you have seen blocks in this chapter that you feel relate to you, you might start your prayer:

*Lord Jesus, I thank You for Your mercy and for once again revealing Your truth to me. Please forgive me for every contact that I have had with any of these works of darkness, especially...*

* * *

"I feel I have learned a great deal about healing, and especially God's mercy, goodness and willing desire to heal me as His child. Is there any thing else I should know?"

# Chapter 17

# Conclusion:
# "Is There Always a Block?"

### Experiential Theology

People like myself, who believe in the Word of God, who believe that the power of God is still available today, and who believe in healing, are often criticized for having "experiential theology." By that my critics mean that I have based my theology upon my own experience, rather than upon the Bible. Those same people will usually refer to some saint in a wheelchair and imply that, if healing was truly available or for everyone, God would certainly have healed that deserving person.

Contrary to their objections, my theology is based not on my own experience of having been healed, or from having personally seen thousands healed, but rather upon **the promises of the Bible**. In addition, I would suggest that the critics are the ones with experiential theology! They base their refutation of healing upon their own observation of (or experience with) individuals in wheelchairs, whom they feel God should have healed, if God were a healer. That is, they allow *their experience* to dictate theology, in blatant conflict with the Word and promises of God.

To repeat an earlier observation, healing is not based upon the goodness of the sick and needy, but rather upon the goodness of God, His inherent nature which desires to help the oppressed, and His faithfulness to His promises.

I myself am presently in a wheelchair, unable to walk as a result of medical mistakes. Objectively speaking, it requires more faith today for me to state that God is a Healer today than it did when I was walking. **But my theology has not changed one iota, nor has God**, since I have been confined to a wheelchair. I believe that I am in the "waiting stages" for this healing. If Jesus healed me of cancer, He can most certainly heal my legs, as I have seen Him do for many people through our ministry over the last thirty years.

I should also explain my theology regarding healing. As I have said, I believe it is always God's will to heal His people.

## Blue Walls or White?

It is as if we went to one wall of this room and scratched away a little of the white paint, and discovered beneath it a layer of blue paint. Then, in turn, we made a scraping on each of the other three walls, and in each case found an undercoat of blue paint. We could then probably correctly conclude that the entire room was once blue, but now it only appears white.

Healing is much the same: we see only a smattering of healing here and there, but the fact of the presence of the smatterings clearly indicate that the *original design was blue*. So it was that the original design of God for His people was healing, but through the centuries as a result of disuse, misuse, abuse and bad teaching...what we see today is a covering up of God's original design!

## Bed "A" *and* Bed "B"

Oftentimes when making a hospital call, the sick individual will say, "Oh Brother Banks, the person in the bed next to me is much sicker than I am, why don't you pray for them, instead?"

226

That is very magnanimous of them, but totally unnecessary. I usually respond, "Brother, we are not going to dim the lights in Heaven by praying for both you and that other person. It won't begin to tax God's strength to heal both of you."

There will not be a power failure caused in Heaven due to our making great demands upon our Omnipotent God! Jesus has the answer to every problem.

As you might suspect, we have ministered to a lot of cancer patients, often being called in at the last moment. As a testimony to God's faithfulness, I am not aware of any of those who actually received ministry, dying with pain. I spent an entire night with one woman who was in the last stages of cancer of the liver. The nurses kept coming in and waking her to see if she wanted any pain medication. She repeatedly said, "No, I have no pain."

I would be lying if I were to state that every person for whom we have prayed in the last thirty years has been healed. Having said that, let me qualify to this extent: we were not able to follow up on every person prayed for, and we were often constrained by time. And this kept us from digging for root blocks to healing, especially in large services.

Many are aware of John G. Lake, the great healing evangelist of the last century, who had over 100,000 recorded healings in his clinic at Spokane, Washington, after a distinguished healing ministry in Africa. The key to Lake's success was that when individuals did not respond to the initial healing ministry, they were taken to counseling rooms and probed to find the *root problems*. The principle of blocks to healing has been drawn out in detail in this book.

Our goal (and expectation) should be one hundred percent success in ministering healing. Kathryn Kuhlman often said, "I hope to conduct a miracle service one day where *everyone* is healed." She recognized that only a small percentage of the thousands who flocked to her meeting were healed, even though she presented a powerful demonstration of both the will, and the power, of God to heal.

About twenty years ago, I was invited to speak for a Ladies Full Gospel meeting in a small town outside St. Louis. The invitation came from a friend, the widow of a judge, named Kathryn. After I spoke, I ministered to forty of the women present, who had problems ranging from dislocated disks to diabetes. All were freed of their symptoms, and I left feeling blessed to have been a part of what God had done.

However, God had a greater blessing in store for me. Kathryn called about six weeks later. She was bubbling over with excitement, "I have just completed a follow-up on every one of the forty women who were healed when you spoke for us....and every single one of them is *still healed*! There have been no reoccurrences of any of the symptoms in over a month!"

What a blessing. Even though the size of my sample was considerably less than that of a Kathryn Kuhlman meeting, one hundred percent of those ministered to were healed! God is still healing today like He did when His Son healed all who were brought to Him.

It is important to recognize that there are different gifts and operations of ministry. I believe that the Holy Spirit normally operates through our ministry in the area of miracles and/or gifts of healings (1 Cor. 12). I do not say that to boast, nor am I entirely comfortable in describing myself in this fashion, because people will misunderstand and assume either that I am deluded, or that I can exercise control over who gets healed, which I cannot. If I could, I would not be in a wheelchair today. I merely function as God's deliveryman, simply functioning as a vessel of the Holy Spirit.

Confusion seems to occur when individuals try to compare themselves or their ministries with those who obviously possess a particular gift, or imply that others should be able to do what they do, in exactly the same way. To illustrate, Kathryn Kuhlman, Benny Hinn, Roxanne Brant and Joan Gieson each operate, or operated, in unique but very similar ways; each has or had a specific kind of anointing as they conducted Miracle services. Often, they just simply announced the healings, which had already taken place elsewhere in the auditorium. Kathryn Kuhlman, for instance, said she never prayed for people to be healed – that "wasn't her ministry." And yet the Holy Spirit was able to do mighty things when she ministered.

Derek Prince used to jokingly complain that Don Basham and Kathryn Kuhlman could "just stroke someone under the chin, and all their demons would come out." In contrast, he had to go through the process and effort of deliverance, the work of actually casting them out one by one. Different anointings, but ultimately the same effect.

Therefore, it isn't particularly helpful for someone with that kind of anointing to tell you "all you have to do is stroke someone under the chin," because it probably won't work for you or me, unless we are operating under the same kind of anointing.

I try to keep my theology pretty simple, so that I can understand it. This is also how God wants us to understand it, as child would (Matt 18:3). For instance,

I believe that God is totally good: good things proceed from Him.

I believe that the Devil is totally evil; all evil comes from him.

I believe that God wills (wants, desires, intends) for all His children to be well.

Therefore, when I do not see in my own experience what I know to be God's will, I have to assume that somehow (even though I may not understand why) the problem is on *this side* of the equation. That is, the problem is mine, and not God's, or that the person ministering healing needs more "tools" for the trade. There is never a power failure in heaven; the problem lies not with the transmitter, but with the receiver.

## IN CLOSING

A final word for those who have been standing on faith for a long time, and may be fighting doubt or discouragement.

This only would I ask of you, "Is God any less able today? Have His promises been diminished by the passage of time?" I hope your answer to these questions is a resounding, NO!

There are no "squatter's rights" for Satan, his diseases, demons, or doubts. I encourage you to cast out, "evict," those doubts now. I urge you to resist those doubts and those fears (that healing isn't for you or that it won't happen to you), just as you would resist any other sin, or temptation.

Remember the basic truth of God's working: **that a delay is not a no!!!**

There is one further reason that you may expect to be healed, last in significance or importance. And this is because the Lord healed me of terminal cancer more than thirty years ago. Had He not done so, you would not be reading this book. But let me make it perfectly clear: the Lord Jesus Christ did not heal me because of any goodness, merit, or virtue on my part; rather He healed me for the same reasons that He healed all those who came to Him two thousand years ago when He walked the streets of the Holy Land.

Then, He was motivated to heal because of *His* goodness, *His* mercy, *His* love, *His* compassion, and *His* desire for the sheep of His own flock to be whole.

He still heals today for exactly the same reasons: He has not lost one iota of that goodness, mercy, love, compassion, and desire for the sheep of His flock to be whole.

**If ever Jesus was a Healer, then He is still a Healer**, **because He is...**

> *Jesus Christ the same yesterday, and to day, and for ever.*                                    Heb. 13:8

**Jesus, is still the same. He is still available today, as our Healer!**

**So, Call upon Him, now!**

> *Beloved, I wish above all things that thou mayest prosper and be in health, even as thy soul prospereth.*
> 3 John 1:2

# APPENDIX A

## HAVE YOU RECEIVED THE BAPTISM WITH THE HOLY SPIRIT?

### God's Old Testament Promise of the Spirit:

*A new heart also will I give you, and a new spirit will I put within you: and I will take away the stony heart out of your flesh, and I will give you an heart of flesh.   And I will **put my spirit within you**, and cause you to walk in my statutes, and ye shall keep my judgments, and do them.*                                                  Ezek. 36:26-27

*And it shall come to pass afterward, that **I will pour out my spirit upon all flesh**; and your sons and your daughters shall prophesy, your old men shall dream dreams, your young men shall see visions:   And also upon the servants and upon the handmaids in those days will I pour out my spirit.*                                      Joel 2:28-29

### Jesus issues an invitation:

*In the last day, that great day of the feast, Jesus stood and cried, saying, If any man thirst, let him **come unto me**, and drink.   He that believeth on me, as the scripture hath said, out of his belly shall flow rivers of living water.   (But this spake he of **the Spirit**, which they that believe on him **should receive**: for the Holy Ghost was not yet given; because that Jesus was not yet glorified.)*
                                                                            John 7:37-39

### Three Scriptural Proofs of Jesus as Baptizer:

*I indeed baptize you with water unto repentance: but he that cometh after me is mightier than I, whose shoes I am not worthy to bear: he **shall baptize you with the Holy Ghost**, an with fire:*
                                                                            Mat. 3:11

233

*And, behold, **I send the promise of my Father** upon you: but tarry ye in the city of Jerusalem, until ye be endued with power from on high.*                                          Luke 24:49

*And John bare record, saying, I saw the Spirit descending from heaven like a dove, and it abode upon him.   And I knew him not: but he that sent me to baptize with water, the same said unto me, Upon whom thou shalt see the Spirit descending, and remaining on him, the same is he **which baptizeth with the Holy Ghost**.*
                                                                  John 1:32-33

## Jesus Issues a Command Concerning the Spirit:
*And, being assembled together with them, **commanded** them that they should not depart from Jerusalem, but wait for the promise of the Father, which, saith he, ye have heard of me.  For John truly baptized with water; but **ye shall be baptized with the Holy Ghost** not many days hence.   But ye shall receive power, after that the Holy Ghost is come upon you: and ye shall be witnesses unto me both in Jerusalem, and in all Judaea, and in Samaria, and unto the uttermost part of the earth.*                     Acts 1:4-5,8

For those who are seeking the Baptism with the Holy Spirit, or who desire more information about it, we recommend the book, *Alive Again!* which is available at any Christian bookstore, or from Impact Christian Books.  Thousands have received just by learning the basic truths and following the simple steps outlined in this book by the same author.

234

# APPENDIX B

## Specific Supernatural Healings in Scripture

God has promised "...*life unto those that find them* [His words], *and* **health to all their flesh!**" (Prov. 4:22)

Since this is true, it is extremely important that the one seeking healing for himself, or for someone else, have a "word from God." It is often especially significant for us to see an instance where God has promised to heal our **specific** disease or affliction; or to see an example in Scripture where our kind of condition was actually healed by Him. For all these reasons we have compiled the following chart to assist you in your own search to meet Him in all His fullness as Healer. May God bless you as you seek Him!

The following table presents specific diseases, afflictions, or conditions which were healed by Jesus Himself, or by other men of God as they were empowered by the Holy Spirit. All, clearly, manifesting God's will to heal His people!

| CONDITION | INSTANCES WHERE HEALED | *Special Promises* |
|---|---|---|
| BARRENNESS | (See Sterility) (See *Del. From Childlessness*) | |
| BLEEDING | Acts 26:8; Matt. 9:20,22; Mark 5:25,29; Luke 8:43,47. | |
| | | ***EZEK 16:6*** |
| BLINDNESS | Matt. 9:27,30 (two blind men) Matt. 11:5; 12:22; 15:31; 20:30,34; 21:14; Mark 8:23,25; 10:46,52; Luke.18:35,43; John 9:1,7; Acts 9:18 | |
| BIRTH | | |
| DEFECTS | John 9:1 (blind) Acts 3:2 (crippled, lame) Acts 14:8,10 (crippled) | |
| CHILDLESSNESS | (See Sterility) | |
| CRIPPLED | Luke 13:11,13; John 5:5,9; Acts 14:8,10.(also see Lame, Birth Defects, Paralysis, Palsy) | |
| DEAFNESS | Matt. 11:5; Mark 7:32,35; 9:25. | |
| DEMONIC | | |
| PROBLEMS | (See Deliverances, below) | |

DIVERSE
  DISEASES          (See All Manner of Sicknesses, below)

DROPSY       Luke 14:2,4

EYE TROUBLE     (See Blindness)

FEVER        Matt. 8:15; Mark 1:31; Luke 4:39; John 4:46,52; Acts
               28:8. (Also see All Manner of Sicknesses, below)

DEATH        I Kings 17:17,22 (Widow's son) II Kings 13:21 (on
               Elisha's bones); Matt. 9:18,25 (Jairus's dau.; 11:5 (the
               dead); Luke 7:12,15 (Widow of Nain's son); 8:42,55;
               John 11:3,4,44 (Lazarus); Acts 9:37,42 (Dorcas); Acts
               14:19 (Paul) 20:9,12 (Eutychus)     ***JOHN 5:21***

DISFIGURED     (See Withered Limbs)

DUMB         Matt. 9:32,33; 12:22; 15:31; Mark 9:25; Luke 11:14.

EPILEPSY     Mark 9:17,ff.

INCURABLE    Mark 5:26

INFERTILITY     (See sterility)(See also *Del. from Childless-*
               *ness*)

INFIRMITY     Luke 13:11,13; John 5:5,9 (See also Unnamed Sick-
               nesses)

HEMORRHAGE    (See bleeding)

LAMENESS    Matt. 11:5; 15:31; 21:14; Acts 3:2; 8:7 (See Crippl-
               ing, Infirmity)

LEPROSY     Numbers 12:10,13,15; II Kings 5:1,14; Matt. 8:3;
               11:1; Mark 1:40,42; Luke 5:12,15; 17:12,15,17

LUNACY      (Lunatic)   Matt. 4:24; 17:15,18.

MAIMED       Matt. 15:31 (See also Disfigured, Severed Limbs,
               Withered Limbs)

MENTAL
  DISORDERS  Matt.4:24;

PALSY        Matt. 4:24; 8:6,13; 9:6; Mark 2:3,12; Luke 5:18,24;
               Acts 9:32,34.

PARALYSIS     (See Palsy)

PLAGUES     Mark 3:10; 5:34; Luke 7:21.

SEVERED          Luke 22:50,51.
  APPENDAGES
SKIN
DISORDERS          (See Leprosy)
SNAKE BITE     Numbers 21:8,9; Acts 28:3,6.
                                            *MARK 16:18, LUKE 10:19*
SPEECH
  IMPEDIMENT Matt. 9:35; 12:22; 15:30,31; Mark 7:32,35; 9:17ff;
                Luke 11:14.
STERILITY      Gen. 17:17ff; 20:17; 21:2; Luke 1:7,13; (See also
                *Del. From Childlessness*)     *PSA. 113:9,ISA. 54:1*
SUICIDAL STATE    Matt. 17:15; Acts 16:27.

WITHERED
  LIMBS          I Kings 13:4-6; Matt. 12:10,13; Mark 3:5; Luke
                6:6,10.

UNNAMED
  SICKNESSES,
UNKNOWN DISEASES,
UNDIAGNOSED,
UNTREATABLE          (See following section)

In addition to the many and varied and specific instances of healing, Jesus and other men of God, (obviously in accordance with the will of God) participated in healing situations wherein entire multitudes were healed of every kind of sickness and disease. This also build our faith...to see so many healed of so much. It also illustrates clearly for us that there are **no ineligible categories** of sufferers, nor any whom God does not will to heal...for surely. if there were such a category, in the wisdom of God there would have been illustrative cases given, or else certainly some poor misguided individual would have brought "an ineligible" to one of Jesus' mass healing services (when they brought all the sick from the surrounding countryside), and Jesus would have had to say, "I'm sorry, Brother, or Sister, but I cannot heal you, for it is not the will of the Father, or you have sinned too greatly, or you are in some other way ineligible." But that **never** happened!

*Every single person who came to Him, or who was brought to Him, was healed without exception!*

237

In light of these facts, consider also the implications of all the following examples of mass healings:

## MULTITUDES HEALED OF
## ALL MANNER OF SICKNESSES AND DISEASES

Matt.    4:23; 8:16; 9:35; 12:15; 14:14; 14:35; 15:30; 19:2;
Mark    1:32; 3:10; 6:5; 6:13; 6:56;
Luke    4:40: 6:17,19; 7:21; 8:23; 9:6; 9:11
John    6:2; Acts 5:16, 8:7; 19:12; 28:9

## MULTITUDES & INDIVIDUALS HEALED and/or DELIVERED,
## FROM TORMENTS, VEXATIONS AND
## OTHER DEMONIC PROBLEMS

Matt.    4:24; 8:16; 8:28; 9:33; 12:22; 15:22,28
Mark    1:26; 1:34, 39; 3:11; 5:2,15; 6:13; 7:25,30; 9:17; 9:38
Luke    4:35; 4:38; 4:41; 6:18; 7:21; 8:2,3; 8:27,33; 9:39,42
Acts    8:7; 16:16,18; 19:12.

AMAZING ANSWERS ABOUT HEALING...

# THREE KINDS OF FAITH FOR HEALING

Many today have been taught that the only way to be
healed is to personally have faith for their healing. It is
implied, one must somehow 'work up' or develop
enough personal *faith-to-be-healed*, and then healing will
come. Many have also been told that the reason they
remain afflicted is because of their lack of faith.

Such statements in addition to being utterly devoid of
compassion, are terribly devastating to the poor hearers.
One could never imagine Jesus saying something so
heartless. Yet these things are often said today. Even
those who have not heard these words spoken aloud
have received them through implication from proud,
spiritually 'superior' friends who believe that these sick
individuals are somehow deficient in faith.

There is good news both for them and for us, because
that teaching is wrong. There are more ways of
being healed than just the one way, as we have been taught.

In this new book, Bill Banks presents a *revelation* of three
main types of faith for healing illustrated in Scripture,
and a fourth which is a combination of the other three.

*Three Kinds of Faith For Healing*          **Paper 4.95**

# ...ABOUT HEALING FROM GOD

**Alsobrook, David**
\_\_\_\_JESUS CHRIST,M.D. The Healing Min of Jesus of Naz.          P  6.95


**Banks,  Bill**
\_\_\_\_ALIVE AGAIN!          P  5.95
\_\_\_\_HOW I WAS HEALED OF CANCER & BAPTISED IN
          THE HOLY SPIRIT  - (1 hr. cassette)          C  4.95
\_\_\_\_THREE KINDS OF FAITH FOR HEALING. . .          P  4.95
\_\_\_\_BREAKING UNHEALTHY SOUL-TIES          P  7.95
\_\_\_\_MINISTERING TO ABORTION'S AFTERMATH          P  5.95
\_\_\_\_POWER FOR DELIVERANCE (Songs of Deliverance)          P  5.95
\_\_\_\_DELIVERANCE FOR CHILDREN & TEENS          P  6.95
\_\_\_\_DELIVERANCE FROM CHILDLESSNESS          P  5.95
\_\_\_\_DELIVERANCE FROM FAT          P  5.95
\_\_\_\_SHAME-FREE          P  7.95


**Bosworth, F.F.**
\_\_\_\_CHRIST THE HEALER          P10.99


**Hagin, Kenneth**
\_\_\_\_HEALING BELONGS TO US          P  3.95
\_\_\_\_KEYS TO SCRIPTURAL HEALING          P  3.95


**Lindsay, Gordon**
  *SERIES ON DIVINE HEALING & HEALTH*
\_\_\_\_HOW YOU CAN HAVE DIVINE HEALTH          P  2.50
\_\_\_\_BIBLE SECRET OF DIVINE HEALTH          P  3.25
\_\_\_\_HOW YOU CAN BE HEALED          P  2.95
\_\_\_\_REAL REASON WHY CHRISTIANS ARE SICK          P  3.95
\_\_\_\_30 BIBLE REASONS WHY CHRIST HEALS TODAY          P  3.50
\_\_\_\_25 OBJECTIONS TO DIVINE HEALING & ANS          P  1.95
\_\_\_\_DIFFICULT QUESTIONS ON DIVINE HEALING          P  1.95
\_\_\_\_....SET OF ABOVE SERIES (7 Titles)          ..........SET 19.00


**Lake, John G.**
\_\_\_\_SERMS/ DOM. OVER DEMONS, DISEASE, DEATH          P  5.95


**Simmons,  Jerry**
\_\_\_\_THAT YE MAY KNOW          P  8.99


SAVE $30.83 - Entire Set of Books ONLY $92.50
+ $5.00 S&H

**IMPACT CHRISTIAN BOOKS**
**332 Leffingwell Ave., Kirkwood, MO 63122  314-822-3309**
*www.Impactchristianbooks.com*

**Impac Chris ian Books**

332 Leffingwell Ave., Suite 101
Kirkwood, MO 63122

AVAILABLE AT YOUR LOCAL BOOKSTORE, OR YOU MAY
ORDER DIRECTLY. Toll-Free, order-line only M/C, DISC,
or VISA 1-800-451-2708.

Visit our Website at *www. impactchristianbooks.com*

**Write for *FREE* Catalog.**